Imprint
Author: Arman Emami
Editor: Gunnar Wagner
Design/Layout: Sagross Design Office GmbH, www.sagross.de

Photo credits:
Page 105, 118, 119: Nico Hesselmann
Page 25: Fotolia 5260351, Author: © Marc Dietrich
Page 27: Fotolia 756506, Author: © Marc Dietrich
Page 28: iStockphoto 12320623, Author: © blende64
Page 30: Fotolia 24862743, Author: © Lucky Dragon USA
Page 31/32: Fotolia 45903204, Author: © tony85
Page 36: Fotolia 3189307, Author: © Miranda Salia
Page 74: iStockphoto 27430110, Author: © Dimijana
Page 74: Fotolia 51032270, Author: © Serg Zastavkin
Page 74: iStockphoto 16337740, Author: © Bo1982
Page 79: iStockphoto 3551617, Author: © apsimo1
Page 110: Fotolia 16534038, Author: © Cpro

DEDICATED TO ALL DREAMERS
WITH A ZEST FOR ACTION

ARMAN EMAMI
360° INDUSTRIAL DESIGN

Contents

Preface

We live in a rapidly changing world that is becoming more complex with every passing second. But what are the challenges resulting from this ever-changing world that concern industrial design?

How important are form, function, haptics and appearance? Is successful design measured by how well it sells or the awards it wins? What should the designer be like? Should the designer be a creative inventor, a pragmatic technician or even an artist? Does it only count when something new is created or is there merit in successfully combining established forms with new innovations? What should the focus be in the future? What makes sense?

One thing is clear: natural resources are getting scarcer and the increasingly intense competition on the world market is forcing designers at large to rethink the design process. Decoration for decoration's sake has become a thing of the past. Fanciful objects like the pretty paper-weight have had their day. Prettiness is no longer enough! Designers working on sustainable products now have to consider the bigger picture and in short: have to optimise design as a multi-disciplinary work.

I have deliberately chosen to write this clearly and concisely. There are enough texts out there using unnecessary jargon, philosophical theories or otherwise setting aims that are not concrete. Instead I will lay out my experiences in practical and daily work as an industrial designer. Additionally, I have tried to combine logic and relevant theories from different fields to create the overall picture that is 360° Industrial Design. Most importantly, this book does not claim to achieve completeness or perfection. "It is better to tackle something imperfectly than to hesitate in perfection".

Arman Emami, Berlin, June 2014

01

THE IDEA

"THE BEST IDEAS ARE A RESULT OF EXPERIENCING
PROBLEMS IN EVERYDAY LIFE."

"Some men see things as they are and ask why.
I dream things that never were and ask why not."

John F. Kennedy

Everything Starts with an Idea

Good industrial design is always preceded by one thing: A great idea. This might sound simple but it's exactly the opposite. In good times an idea will appear out of thin air, yet more often than not it is elusive: A diva waiting to be courted before coming up with the goods. The better one understands how an idea emerges, the easier an idea can be coaxed out of its shell.

The Idea Behind the Idea

Ideas actually do grow on trees – or at least the first approaches do. You can find them wherever you are: On the bus, on your way to work, during breakfast or in the shower. You just need to know what to look for, how to recognise the signs. One easy way is not to ignore the problems of everyday life any longer but to observe and embrace them. Having done that you can start to find intelligent and practical solutions. If you are lucky this starts intuitively and on its own. Intuition is a key aspect in creative design and developing processes. It emerges from the subconscious and intellect then just has to follow and act on the impulse.

But what to do when intuition is not available on tap? One way is a structured search for solutions. There is no master key that opens every door, but a systematic thinking process is a starting point.

Abstraction

Concentrating on the essentials.
The first step is recognizing the essentials. The process is like peeling an onion: The more layers are peeled away the closer a designer gets to the centre of all things. With the idea stripped bare, the designer is able to see the foundations of the design more clearly:
Free from clutter.

Analytic Thinking

Knowledge helps to reshape things.
It is very important to systematically analyze facts and circumstances, to dissect and fractionalize them. What functions well and what might disturb a smooth performance? What can be changed and how? It is about acquiring the tools to literally find that needle in the haystack.

Bionics

How to shape a discovery into an invention.
Nature already has the answers to many problems, proven over millennia. You just need to know where to look. Bionics is exactly this search tool. It adapts the achievements of the living environment for a technical implementation process. Evolution offers incredible insights and best-of intelligent systems that win over less effective solutions in the end. But nonetheless that does not mean we should stop being creative ourselves.

There are basically two differences between products formed by nature and those that are man-made. An essential difference is the fact that nature mostly uses materials produced by organic living sources. In addition, many of nature's creations only function as long as they are alive. Take for example the Tyrannosaurus Rex, an impressive beast, but belonging to a now extinct species. The only existing dinosaurs today are puzzled together from dead bone fragments and made of plastic or else roaming cinematic landscapes. Biological systems therefore, have naturally imposed constraints. For example: All the separate parts of an organic system must be connected to one another to guarantee energy and nutrient input. Another constraint lies in the fact that organic compounds cannot withstand high temperatures. There are therefore, as far as we know, no jet-propelled eagles in the skies. By using non-organic materials engineers can create objects that do not and cannot exist in nature.

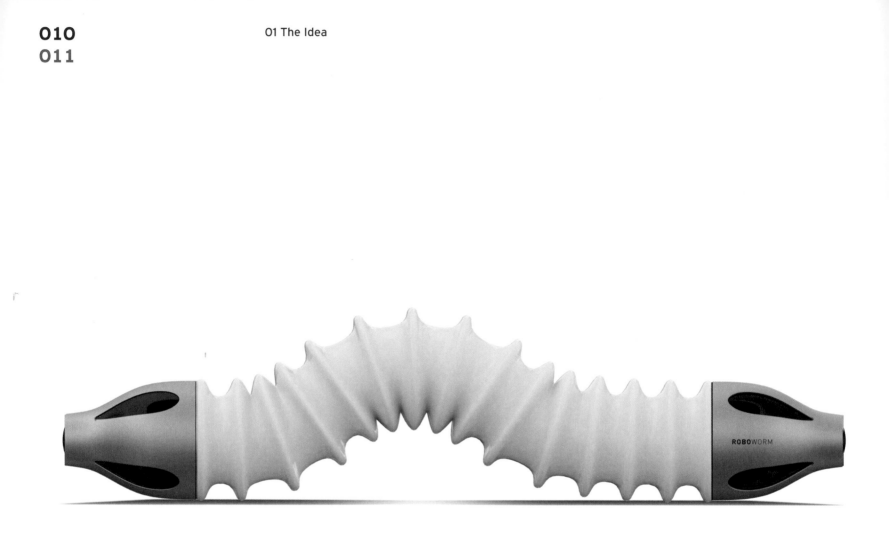

Robo Worm

This robot mirrors the movements of a caterpillar. The motions of the caterpillar's circular muscles are simulated through the controlled magnetisation of metal rings integrated into a silicone tube. The construction enables the Robo Worm to move on rough and uneven surfaces found in canals and tunnels. Even where chain wheels and other traditional means of transportation get caught, the Robo Worm contorts itself without problems.

Robo Worm has two heads, one at each end, making it possible to move backwards without having to flip over. This principle enables backwards movement even in very tight shafts. Robo Worm is equipped with cameras and additional sensors, for example a microphone, to make recordings possible even in hard-to-reach areas. The recordings can be sent to a receiving station immediately or stored in the device for later extraction.

Have you ever wondered why nature never invented the wheel? There is one possible reason: For a freely turning wheel, there can be no fixed connection to the other components. In a living organism, rotating parts are therefore impossible to supply with blood and energy. That is something simply unachievable. It took the inventive mind of human beings to create 'dead' matter like steel or plastic which enables us not only to build engines, axes and wheels but to drive on highways at maximum speed, easily reaching the 155 mph mark. Humans might not have more fascinating possibilities to create new things than nature itself, but we do have other means. Furthermore, humans sometimes have completely different problems than nature does. As a result we cannot turn to nature for the solution to all our problems. We have to solve some of them on our own! Despite our enthusiasm for bionics, we must also remember our own strengths and learn how to make the most of them.

Overcoming Clichés

Thinking out of the box is a must.
First of all, it is important to free ourselves from outdated and narrow thinking. Development needs change; it is the basis for all progress. But likewise it is necessary to recognize that not every cliché is necessarily a bad thing. Design is an evolution, so today's achievements are the result of a long-term process. Of course you can develop a wheel further, but to be honest, no one needs an angular shaped wheel. Do not try to be different at all costs! A change should always be for the better. Sadly this is not always the case, with many products ignoring already existing concepts that work and are valuable. In some cases products are marketed as newly designed just to sell more and effective branding masks the lack of actual improvement. People might remember Hans Christian Andersen's fairy tale "The Emperor's New Clothes" where tailors pretend to sew new clothes for the king that only the clever and witty will be able to see. In the end the emperor walks around naked because the new clothes are only a massively successful marketing campaign that everybody wants to believe in order not to appear stupid. The same applies to design that loses contact with the product and is used simply as a merchandising tool. So in principle design is easy: Keep the good things but be open-minded towards new ideas.

Design Concept Versus Solutions

Not every idea is a good design concept. There is a clear difference between designers and inventors. In one way every designer is a kind of inventor, this on the other hand does not mean every inventor knows how to design and create. For example: On January 29, 1886 Karl Benz filed a patent application for the first petroleum driven car. Even though he was an extraordinary inventor, his three-wheeled vehicle was barely more than a naked frame: A tricycle that drove. The design concept came later. So, what is the key difference between a designer and an inventor? Only if the form and design are part of a solution can one truly speak of a design concept.

Even designs earning prominent awards often do not value this aspect enough. Suddenly innovative technical developments made by technicians and engineers are celebrated as innovative designs as well – although the concept has barely anything to do with actual design.

One can, for example, ask why a well-regarded design competition was won by an ultra flatscreen TV. Of course it is an understandable approach to make a television screen as flat as possible, and new developments in LCD- and LED-technology have finally made such a design feasible after years of research. But the designer was never the catalyst or trigger for a flat screen design, he only took care of the appealing packaging. It looks nice, but product design can be so much more than simply creating beautiful things. When the product embodies the main part of a solution through its design, something unexpected and new can suddenly emerge.

"A design concept means giving shape to an idea."

USB-Clip

USB devices are getting smaller every day. And we still like to send pen drives via mail. But since they tend to be rather small they can get lost easily. A good choice therefore is the USB clip that can be attached to any kind of document like business cards, letters, leaflets or brochures no matter how thick the paper. Three lamellae generate a good adhesion. The USB-clip connects analogue papers with digital information and is therefore a reliable and valuable assistant for correspondence in our times.

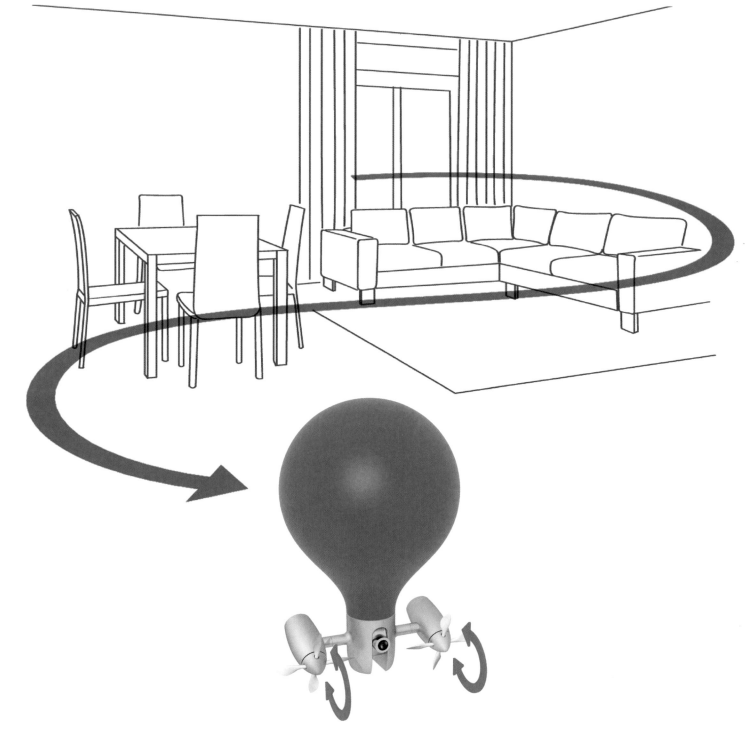

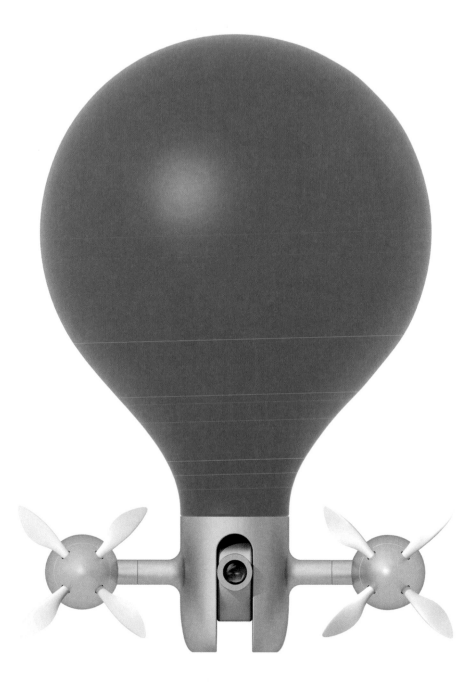

Zipper
is a flying camera and recording device for indoor use. It uses the principle of a gas balloon combined with propellers steered by a fine mechanical motor. This allows you to navigate the Zipper quickly and silently through closed rooms without consuming much energy. Additionally the device has excellent maneuverability.

Fields of application:
• **Movie production: unrestricted camera operation**
• **Security: Video control of hard to reach areas like cable funnels and canalization**
• **Private use: Webcam, childcare, toy**

02

FUNCTIONALITY AND USABILITY

"EVERY DESIGN SOLUTION HAS TO PROVE ITSELF ON A DAILY BASIS."

"God never lets a goat's tail grow longer than needed."

German Proverb

The Question of If and How

There is a difference between "doing the right things" and "doing things right." Creating well-functioning and easy-to-handle products is, of course, one of the responsibilities of industrial design. At the same time, a new concept should not only be effective but also efficient.

Functionality

It works well.
What distinguishes a product that satisfies users? It has to function without any problems. If it can achieve this one thing it is already a useful product. This might sound self-evident but is far less common than one might think.

This aspect clarifies whether a thing actually works or not. In product design something is functional if it fulfills a certain task as it should. A hairdryer is functional if it dries hair, as is a bicycle that can be ridden and a razor that gets rid of the stubble on a man's chin. The question of how well an object fulfills its task is a question of usability: its suitability for use.

Usability

The degree of usefulness.
The German standard: DIN EN ISO 9241-11 is not really a user-friendly definition and yet it defines product usability. It is present on products and software found to be: Effective, efficient and satisfactory. As user-satisfaction results from efficiency, effectiveness and a few other factors we can immediately delete the word 'satisfactory' from our memories and replace it with 'practicability.' But more on that later, first we are going to have a quick look at two aspects: Effectiveness and efficiency.

Effectiveness

Something is effective whenever the desired target is reached. For example, finding a parking space in the centre of London is quite effective no matter how long it takes. But if the search has lasted for hours and wasted gallons of gas that would not be very efficient at all. For gaining effectiveness in comparison to efficiency only the result counts - but not the effort it took. To be able to evaluate effectiveness from a design perspective one has to be a little bit more careful. A lack of effectiveness is not always the result of bad design. Take for example a razor: If it does not work properly the cause might not be bad design but could also be a technical issue or construction related.

"In design the combination of effectiveness and efficiency is the ideal."

Efficiency

Efficiency is the golden calf everyone dances around. And not without reason – it is the relation between effort and result. The question is: What is necessary to achieve a certain goal, how economical is it and will it pay off? The less the input and effort, the more efficient the result.

Effort means various things. Essential factors are the time, the energy and the concentration needed to be invested in achieving the goal. An outstandingly clear industrial design, for example, can reduce the time and concentration necessary for handling a tool and thereby improve its efficiency.

Practicability

What characteristics does a mobile phone need to make it valuable? It needs to fit into a pocket and should not be too big or cumbersome. And what about a mobile storage device? It needs to be protected against potential damage from being dropped or falling out of a bag. These are things that could be categorized under practicability. This is a criterion even harder to grasp than efficiency and effectiveness because what is perceived as practical is, often enough, an individual decision and can be subjective.

In general it can be said: Practicability means suitability for daily use. This can include aspects like compactness, stackability or transportability which makes us perceive of something as practical. Other points on the positive scale are high reliability and useful additional functions. Extravagant design can often sacrifice practicability for effect. What is the use of an elaborately designed product if it is far too bulky or easy to break? The design has rendered the product impractical.

Locko
Outdoor water taps installed in gardens or open spaces leave themselves vulnerable to the threat of being turned on an unauthorized third person who might cause flooding or water damage. Locko uses a number lock mechanism and therefore offers a useful and practical outdoor solution that is easy to implement.

Steward

Steward is an all-in-one mouth care set – a complete entity consisting of toothbrush, toothpaste, mouth rinse and dental floss. The handle is used to store capsules filled with various substances like toothpaste or mouth rinse. Brush heads, dental floss spindle and capsules can be refilled and replaced individually. Steward's design refrains from sharp edges or cracks, to avoid dentifrice residues and makes the mouth care set easy to clean.

Integrating Products Into Everyday Life

"It is unfortunate that products become analyzed in a closed system."

No product exists in an empty space. Only its usage in everyday life shows the value of a product: How useful it is and how well it fits into our life.

Every product has a social compound. No matter how well it functions it also has to be integrated into its natural surroundings. For this reason, in a design process it helps to look at and analyze product interaction: Which items will the product come into contact with in its daily life?

Just imagine a USB flash drive: Conceptualized to transport data easily and designed to be carried around all the time – just like a key ring. So why not combine these two things in a practical union? A pen drive that can be securely attached to a key ring is always at hand – You won't have go looking for the thing anymore: A simple but practical combination that spares users not only time but nerves as well.

Compactness

"Space is gold. Sometimes we have to fight for every millimeter."

The most compact geometrical form is a sphere. From a mathematical point of view a sphere has a maximum volume combined with a minimal surface. Therefore, it is no surprise that every planet is spherical. But does this mean every product should be designed like this as well? Hardly practical.

Compact forms should be tailored according to the function of a product. At the same time feasibility cannot be neglected - particularly with complex products it is helpful to calculate the volume of the different parts involved. Then the various volumes can be combined with each other, like in a complex puzzle resulting in the most compact total capacity. That compactness can be a key factor for success has been proven by the design of the famous Swiss pocketknife, which combines a multiplicity of different practical tools in a very small space. This has made the pocketknife a huge export success. The trick is quite simple: The knife is this compact because every element can be folded and stored inside it. The same principle can work with other products as well. Space can be saved with telescopic constructions, swing out mechanisms, interfolding designs and other flexible systems. Just imagine if we could not fold together an umbrella and so reduce it to a small part of its original size!

close

open

Loopo - a practical connection

The storage space on pen drives is constantly improving and at the same time the devices are becoming ever smaller. Often enough they get lost in bags or during transport. A solution for this problem could be to attach it to other objects like a key ring. Therefore, USB devices often have an additional strand or chain. Not so with Loopo: the pen drive has an integrated orbital clasp with a spring construction to make attaching the USB flash drive to other objects easy to handle.

If umbrellas were not foldable, we can only assume that we would probably get wet in the rain quite often because not everybody would carry an umbrella around due to its bulky shape and size. Another example of compactness in everyday life are chairs that can be stacked when not in use. Even though this has nothing to do with the intended and normal use of chairs, this heightens the practicability of the product by making it easy to save space.

Combination of Functions

"Different functions have to match each other for a lifetime."

There are 2-in-1 shampoos, 2-in-1 notebook bags, 2-in-1 coats and many other 2-in-1 variations. To unite two different functions in one product has become a trend in recent years. The user enjoys buying only one instead of two products for a purpose: Saving money and space. Additionally, the combination of functions reduces the production and material expenses because the common components are just required once.

But there is always a catch somewhere. No wonder that there are still no combinations like a device that includes a razor and a mobile phone, or office chairs that can be used as beds, or toothbrushes with a voice recording function: A combination has to make sense. Both functions should somehow be compatible with each other.

Before joining two functions into one product remember the maxim: Marry in haste, repent at leisure. In other words never reduce the quality of a compound because in design, unlike math, two half things combined do not necessarily make a whole.

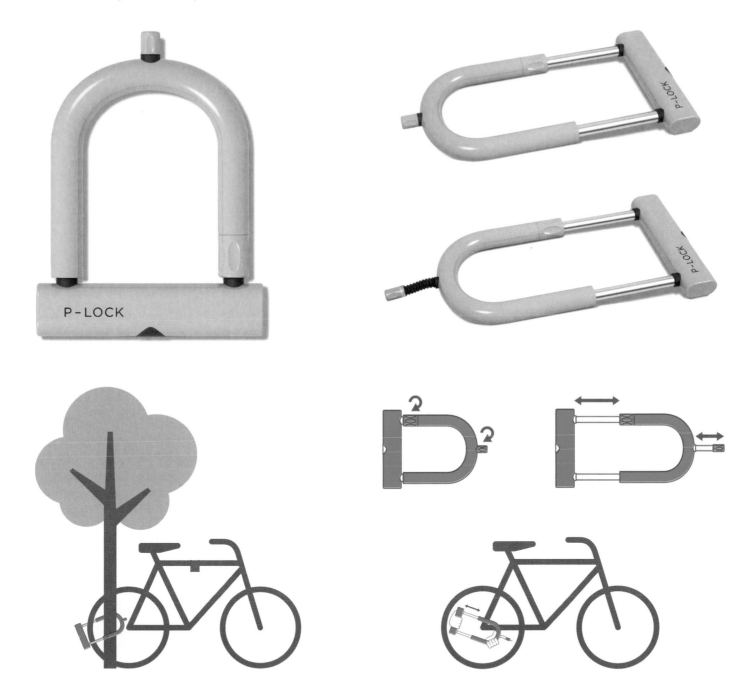

P-Lock

Cyclists are often in need of two things: A bicycle lock and a bicycle pump. Cycle pumps often get stolen because they cannot be secured when the bike is parked and locked. P-lock combines both items and therefore has a few advantages:

1) the cyclist only has to carry one item instead of two.

2) the bicycle pump will be locked to the bike when left behind and therefore secured against theft.

While pumping, the form has an ergonomic advantage since the bow can be held in the hand making it possible for the other hand joint to be constant and perpendicular to the direction of movement.

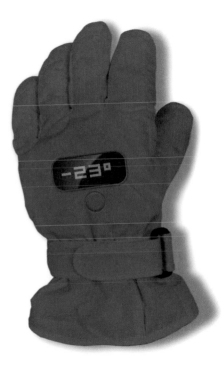

Time   **Heart Rate**   **Temperature**

Timeout

In winter, especially when doing winter sports like skiing, it is hard to read a watch hidden under long sleeves and gloves. Timeout offers a solution by showing a digital display on the back of a glove, making telling the time quite easy. With a simple touch of a button Timeout also displays other relevant information like the wearer's heart rate or the temperature. It is also possible to integrate a GPS tracker or a stopwatch. Using an OLED (organic light emitting diode) display means low energy consumption; the small button battery will last for many years.

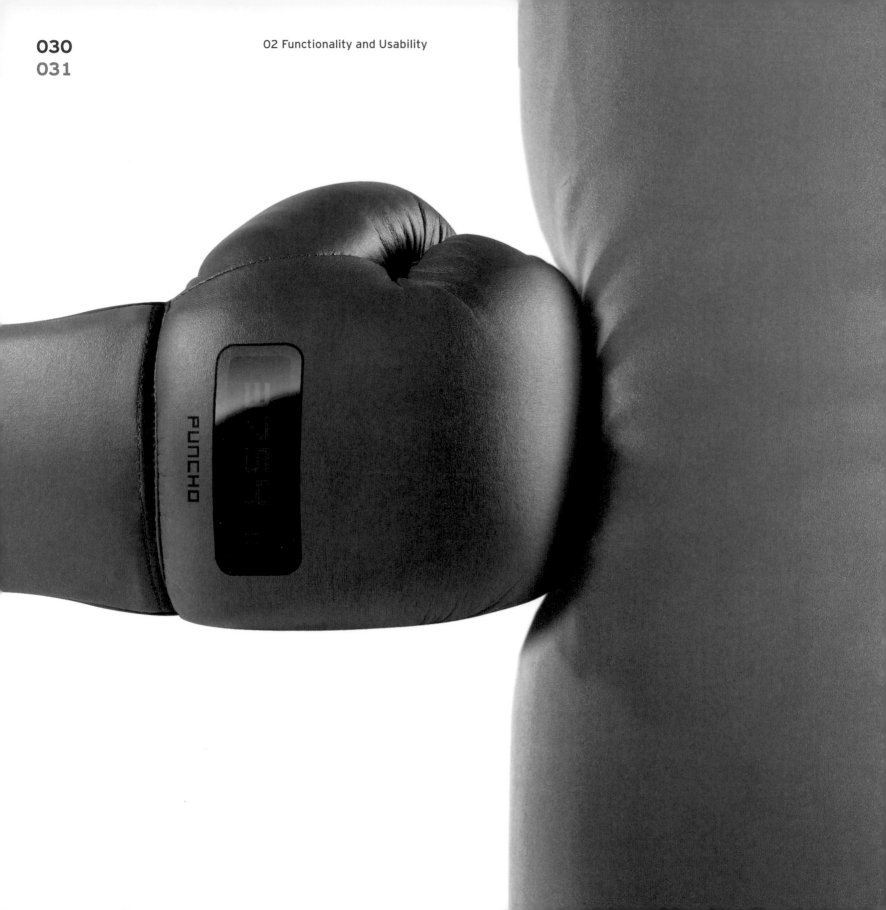

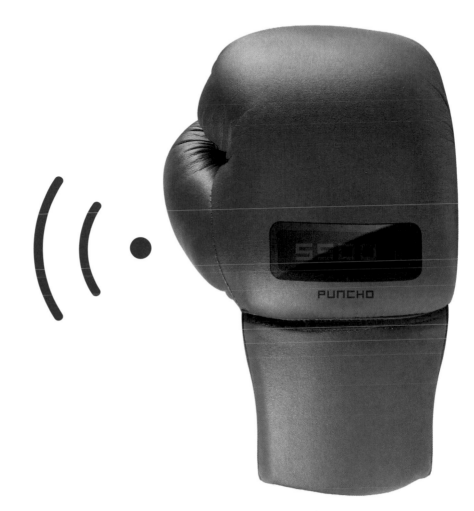

Puncho
is an intelligent boxing glove. It supports athletes and helps them make progress via measuring the force and speed of the punches. A flexible screen based on OLED- technology visualizes the results. It comes with a specially developed app, that allows the user to not only measure their own progress but to compare their results with other athletes.

Easy Cleaning

"High gloss casing and fingerprints are a mismatched duo."

Luckily our world is not as clean as many design catalogues would have us believe. After a very short time many products no longer look as glamorous as they did when new. Thinking about the effects of usage on a product before creating a design can avoid product degradation and user disappointment.

Generally there are a few points to consider:

Surfaces
Prevent unnecessary unevenness.
Smooth surfaces attract far less dirt and are far easier to clean. Decorative elements like grooves, holes, pores or waves do not only attract the attention of the viewer but also dust. One example: Many toothbrush handles have distinctive grooves, to give the impression they are easier to handle – a pseudo-function to distinguish it from other products in the same category. It really is a mystery how generations of teeth brushers managed to get by without the toothbrush slipping out of their hands before this incredible innovation came along. In reality, instead of actually providing a better grip, grooved handles only function as a magnet for toothpaste residue. Rest assured: A toothbrush without grooves will not be doomed to spend its life on the floor.

Finishing
Give dirt no chance.
If you closely monitor smartphone users, you will often enough see them frantically wiping the screens and surfaces with their sleeves. A sign of their helpless and hopeless attempts to clean their fingerprints from the glass casing. Only that each attempt adds a new smear to the screen. With matt, sandblasted surfaces this problem could easily be solved. Dirt-repellent finishes keep products attractive for a long time.

Sometimes the so-called lotus effect could help: Dirt will simply drip off the surfaces. The principle was first discovered with the Asian lotus flower and today is used to keep the surfaces of clothes, cars and various other items dirt free, among them the glass façades of buildings.

See the explanation in the appendix
on page 149.

NO K.O. is a milk frother that not only looks good but also solves a specific problem: Its bounce-back ability prevents it from toppling over and rolling away. It needs little space and always leaves a tidy impression. The half round steel bottom with a low center of gravity always returns NO K.O. to the standing position on its own. Edges and grooves were purposely omitted in the design. The result is a device that looks good and is also easy to clean.

Color and material
Suitably dressed.
To clean your cellar dressed all in white is impractical, to say the least. This principle can be applied to products. Sections that come into contact with dirt should be geared to these needs. Darker colors optically absorb dirt and make it nearly invisible. Smooth surfaces help to prevent dust and dirt from gaining a foothold in the first place. Extra layering can also stop foreign particles from getting lodged into surfaces and damaging their look.

In other words: A product should not only look new when fresh from the factory, but also look fresh after years in use.

Ergonomics

People should feel comfortable enough to use certain products. Ergonomics is the science of optimizing the usability of devices. The term originates in the Greek words ergon (work or deed) and nomos (law, rule). Considering that most products are designed for human use, it is quite logical to adapt products to a human's needs – and not the other way round. With many products this does not seem to be the case. But why? Either ergonomic aspects are not seriously taken into consideration if at all, or many products are geared towards a core target group and a fine-adjustment does not seem profitable enough. Bad times for individualists.

Because humans are not only made of flesh and blood but also spirit and mind, ergonomics have to address two aspects – one physical and one mental.

"Products are made for mankind - not the other way around."

Handycan
The collapsible form makes beverage cans easier to recycle. This minimizes not only transportation costs to the recycling stations but also the costs for storage in advance. The width and radius of the can's grooves are adjusted to the average finger size – for easier handling and a better grip.

Physical Ergonomics

Here human anatomy is clearly in the foreground. The physical ergonomics looks at the relations between humans and machines and optimizes product usability and handling. Even if you only think of ten people in your own circle of acquaintances, you will understand how hard it is to please everybody. Although there might be no panacea, there are certain methods that help to create good ergonomics.

Adaptation to the Average

Often it fits – often enough it does not.
This method functions well with many products, but has disadvantages as well since there are always people outside the norm. Therefore these solutions are not optimal for every user. To give a good example: In automotive design the interior is constructed for a person with an average height of 1,70 metres. This reflects the average size of people all over the world. Too bad that people in the middle and northern regions of Europe are a bit taller than that: Here the average height is 1.80 metres. But adjusting car interiors to this size would reduce the sales figures in Asia and the Americas. Even the German automobile industry does not take the height of its fellow countrymen into account.

Adjustable Constructions

Better, but more expensive.
With this strategy the differences of product users are taken into account. For example: Height-adjustable computer screens. Every user can change the screen according to his or her height. Often enough producers opt to not take advantage of these sorts of options because, as mentioned above, of the additional costs. Instead they focus on an average value and deliberately give up on the small percentage that don't fit into this standard. When considering a flexible construction, the decision is dependent on how well a non-adjustable construction suits the target group and how expensive its realization is.

Flexible Solutions

Naturally individual.
This approach uses flexible materials and intelligent constructions to automatically adjust products to different situations. This saves a lot of time and effort. The adjustments normally happen continuously without any limitations or settings. In this field there are many good examples originating in living nature that have been developed by bionics. This might be the future in ergonomics: Smooth, individual automatic adjustments. The car seat constructions of Thomas Klawitter show how far such innovations could go: The designer and his team of engineers at BMW based his bionic seats on the anatomy and skeleton construction of trout. They have a clever body feature: When pushing against the side of a trout's body the fin moves in the opposite direction. The same effect is used for the backs of car seats: When a human body is pressed into the seat due to higher speeds or curves the backrest automatically tightens its grip on the driver's body and gives it better support. Additionally the headrest moves towards the head. Thanks to the bionics-based construction the innovative seat is not only very comfortable, but also lighter than other models. The smaller build also leaves more space for people sitting in the back.

Mental Ergonomics

This area is far less researched than the physical ergonomics of products. There are no one-fits-all patent solutions for this either. How people handle information, for example, is researched through perception and cognitive psychology. There is an important difference between what people see and what they later recognise, therefore the mental ergonomics are as important as the physical. For instance: When a person looks at a tree, the plant projects thousands of individual leaves on a man's retina. He, however, does not see individual leaves but sees the tree in its entirety. Relevant brain research has proven particularly useful in optimizing cognitive ergonomics and is often applied, among other things, to interface design.

"There is no catch-all solution for every product."

A practical application for mental ergonomics

Imagine you have to depict the numbers 0 to 12 not in numbers but bars. Smaller numbers like 4 and 5 can be pictured easily and without error. With the larger amounts more mistakes appear; the error rates increase in proportion to the visualized number. Dividing the numbers into smaller groups gives a better outline and provides a faster and more accurate readout. The Neolog watch uses this simple principle and visualizes time in its natural form. Even though it shows each minute it stays concrete and objective. Time is divided into hours, ten-minute steps and minutes. Thanks to groupings of three the time can be read quite easily.

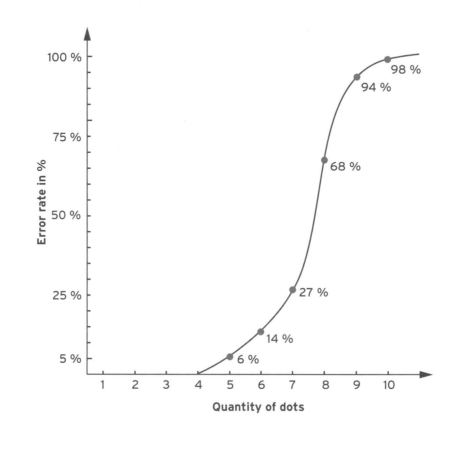

In this study 200 members of a test study were asked to recognise a certain amount of objects without numbering. The error rate grew steadily after the subjects were shown five or more objects.

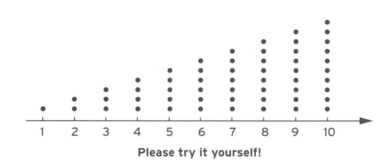

Neolog
The time is shown in amounts without being abstract. The perception of the neologian scale is like that of an hourglass, but additionally is very precise and fast to grasp. Depicted time: 6:24.

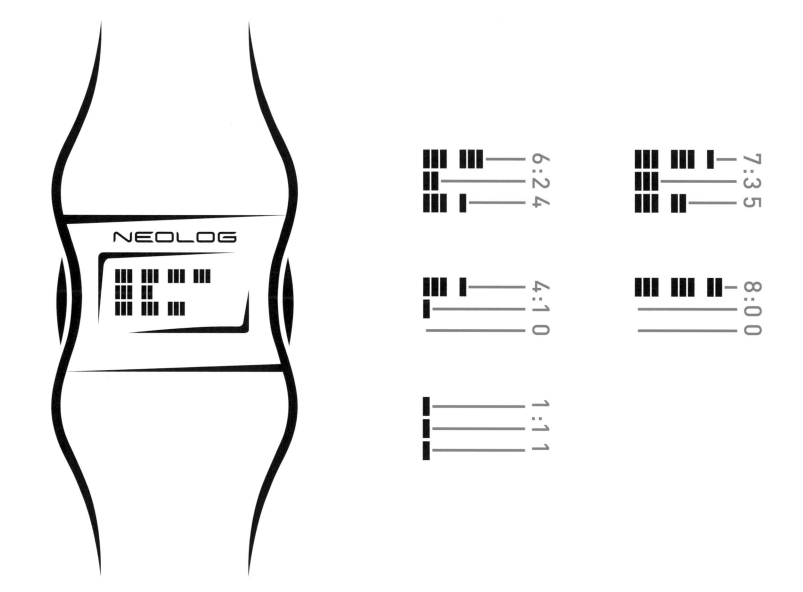

Neolog OS

visualizes the time – beyond cultural and language barriers. Time is shown as a quantity. Hours, ten-minute steps and minutes are depicted in groups of bars. For better accountability the bars are subdivided in groups of three.

Once the wearer gets used to it the display provides an unusual and instinctive grasp of time.

Are mental ergonomics the same for everyone? No. Many of our features have been developed over centuries of evolution; people have certain common characteristics all over the world. Nonetheless, cognitive ergonomics are a flexible part of the creation of products since every human being is the result of his or her individual experiences. No study in the world could hope to gather all this data, so it remains something personal. The basis for these experiences lies in an individual's biography and cultural background. The cultural aspect can at least be taken into consideration. Just imagine designing a dining table for the Asian market. Then it would be good to know that people in these cultural circles prefer to sit on the floor while eating. The personal aspects are of course far more complex and can only be guessed at. Next to the normal adjustment possibilities a subsequent flexible adaptation to the user's preferences plays an important role. Therefore measuring and regulation techniques for individual behavior and a systematic adaptation in the design process are necessary. Good examples of this can be found in newly developed musical apps. These small programs learn more and more information about the music preferences and habits of users. This allows for the creation of individual playlists and a generation of suggestions for similar music. It is a possible that these apps will one day know us better than we know ourselves.

03 AESTHETICS

"AESTHETICS IS THE POETRY IN THE LANGUAGE OF FORMS."

"Beauty will save the world."

Fyodor Dostoevsky, from the novel "The Idiot"

Accounting for Taste

Is it really true that beauty lies in the eye of the beholder? Can beauty be universally defined? Is beauty relative or absolute? There are many indications that beauty in nature exists separate from the individual's perception - it is far less subjective than often thought. In nature everything makes sense: But what sense lies in beauty, what function does it have? According to evolutionary theory all matter strives towards perfection. Is beauty therefore a motor for development, a necessary wheel in the clockwork of nature to reach perfection? And why are we so fascinated and addicted to beauty? Why do we blindly follow in its wake? Could a greyer, duller world not be acceptable? Whatever intelligence is behind creation it could have also created it with a bit more pragmatism. To be honest functionality does not need beauty, the world could have functioned on logical principles without any beauty included. So why does beauty exist? And why does it count so much in our lives? One explanation might be that beauty is not a method for development but part of the intended perfection. Beauty is universally objective, beyond the human. Symmetry and the golden section are a given and are as much a part of nature as gravity or acoustic waves. Of course personal factors always play an important role as well when speaking about beauty. Everybody has his or her own tastes which makes beauty quite subjective. What someone defines as beauty depends on a person's biography, social surroundings and biological abilities. A color-blind person sees the world differently than someone who sees every tiny nuance of color. Someone who always wears tailored suits might have a problem with torn jeans and t-shirts.

Ideals of beauty vary. But if we can set aside our personal preferences we can find a common denominator. And then why not take taste into consideration.

Form

In everyday life the creativity of industrial designers is curtailed by definite limits. For a start form follows function only to a certain degree; the second barrier is the manufacturing process. But let us put that aside for a bit and focus on aesthetics.

What are the elementary rules?

Harmony

Detailing similarities

The composition of a new design is like creating a visual form of music. If the designer can connect the single notes it becomes a harmony. The same applies to optics. Human visual perception functions according to the following principles: Our eyes are constantly sending new information to our brain, this flood of stimuli is sorted and important and unimportant facts are separated. Without this filter our brain would be hopelessly over-saturated – as would we.

Information that has been filtered is then sent to a so-called 'database of memories' where it can be cross-referenced with information already stored there. We understand a seen object and a copy of its form emerges before our inner eye. What we see therefore is not reality but a reproduction of reality.

The more easily our brains are able to analyze a form, the more pleasant and enjoyable the experience of the analysis. Too many details, bad proportions and unfamiliar forms make this procedure far more difficult and can make objects appear disharmonious and awkward. But if the brain finds logical coherences in a form and is not strained by too many unnecessary details, reconstruction becomes easier. The object seems more harmonious and we have greater pleasure looking at it. It is logical and optimal to reproduce an object in a way our brain can easily comprehend.

At this point it is worth looking more closely at the measures that need to be taken to develop harmonious design:

"It is amazing how complete is the delusion that beauty is goodness."

Nikolajewitsch Leo Tolstoy

Consistency

The fewer different forms the better.

The visualization of a product is facilitated if and when the same radius is used every time, the same operating elements are present and other similar factors are present.

Proportions

Relieving the brain.
When looking at an object your brain automatically analyzes the mathematical proportions of the various components whether you like it or not. The composition either feels elaborate, the division of lengths and distances harmonious, or not. Consistent proportions therefore do not please the eye but the brain.

The golden section.
Finding the ideal formula for setting forms together in harmony has occupied mankind since time began. That this quest is worth it can be seen, amongst other things, in the Golden Section. As early as circa 300 BC the Ancient Greek mathematician Euclid of Alexandria outlined the principle for the first time. A Franciscan monk with the impressive name of Luca Paciola di Borgo San Sepolcro characterized the Golden Section as a godly division. The first concrete description of it was made by professor Michael Maestlin in Tübingen: In 1597 he defined it in a letter to his former student Johannes Kepler as approximately 1.6180340. To bring a bit more color to the rather dull theory please imagine the task is to color a set of bars in two different colors, one part in orange and the other in grey.

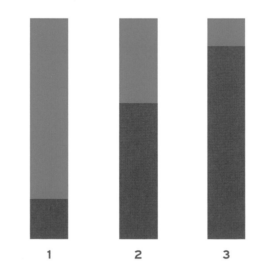

1   2   3

When is the proportion between both parts the most harmonious for you?

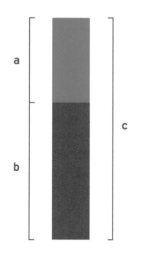

Why actually does the second composition seems to be the most harmonious? Let us take a closer look. The orange part has a length of **a** and the grey area of **b**. Comparing **a** and **b** with the entire length of **c** we find that: The relation of **a** to **b** is the same as that of **b** to **c**. This describes the ideal partition ratio:

If you divide a length according to the Golden Section the proportions of both sections to one another correlate exactly to the proportion of the larger section to the total length. The ratio is 1 : 1.618...

$$\varphi = \frac{a}{b} = \frac{b}{c}$$
$$\rightarrow \varphi = \frac{a}{b} \rightarrow a = \varphi \, b$$

$$\rightarrow \frac{a}{b} = \frac{b}{a+b}$$
$$\rightarrow \varphi = \frac{b}{c} = \frac{b}{a+b}$$

$$\rightarrow a^2 + a\,b = b^2$$
$$\rightarrow \frac{\varphi}{1} = \frac{b}{\varphi b + b}$$

$$\rightarrow a^2 + a\,b - b^2 = 0$$
$$\rightarrow \varphi^2 b + \varphi b = b$$

$$\rightarrow \varphi^2 b + \varphi b - b = 0$$

$$\rightarrow \varphi = \frac{1 \pm \sqrt{5}}{2} \qquad \varphi = 1,618 \ \text{ or } \ \phi = -0,618$$

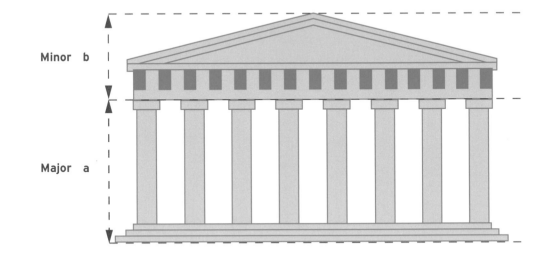

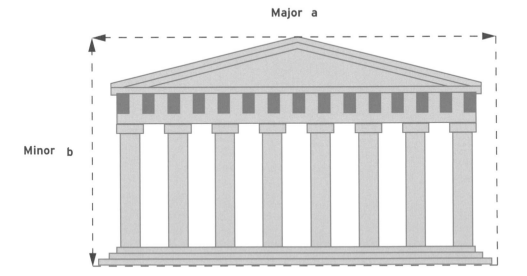

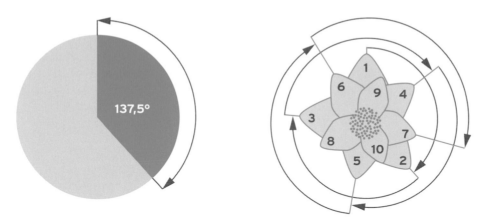

The angle between successive florets in some flowers is the Golden Angle.

The Golden Angle

The Golden Angle is obtained when the circumference of a circle is divided according to the ratio of the Golden Section. The subsequent angle measures 137,5° and is designated as the Golden Angle. As you move around and use the Golden Angle in rotation, you will reach new positions every time that are relatively proportioned. This effect occurs because you cannot divide a full circle of 360° by portions of 137,5°. If you keep adding on portions, the result will be an offset pattern. Those patterns you see in nature and only nature are proof that the Golden Angle is imbedded in LIFE.

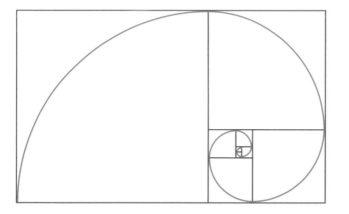

The Golden Spiral

The Golden Spiral (approximated by means of quarter circles) is defined through a sequence of quarter circles, the radius of which is increased by a factor of 1.68.

This division ratio can be found in the proportions of many buildings as well as in paintings, layouts and even music. But what is more interesting is the fact that even in nature many proportions rely on the same principle.

Layout Grid

Keeping Order "behind the scenes".
All elements in design are oriented towards an invisible layout grid so that their allocation leads to a harmonious overall impression. Next to the visible elements like displays, control knobs or vent holes, imaginary objects like circle centers or outer line extensions are subordinate to a layout grid. This is not only positive for a product's look but also for its usability, as a clear structure in design is easy to grasp and use intuitively. Most often a quadratic space is used for the layout grid, so the elements are adjusted horizontally and vertically. Beyond this there are further possibilities: instead of quadratic grids, those divided into triangles offer great new opportunities for arranging the elements. Even circular grids and grids based on geometrical algorithms are possibilities.

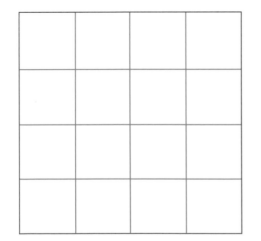

quadratic grid

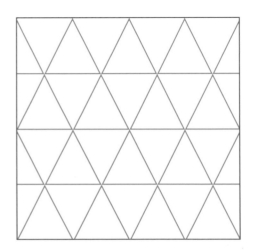

triangular grid

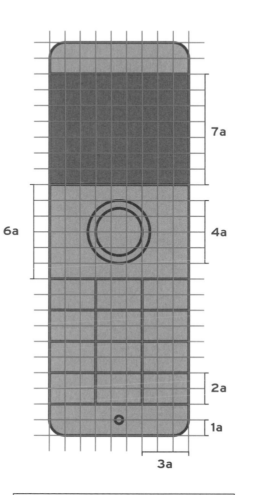

This example shows how elements like displays and operating buttons are adjusted to an invisible layout grid.

7a

6a   4a

2a

1a

3a

imaginary points
The radius centre of this rounded corner is also positioned according to the grid.

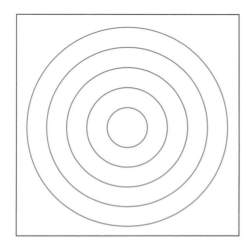

radial rasterization

archimedean helix

Arrangement of dimples on the
surface of a pestle (complete illustration on page 105).

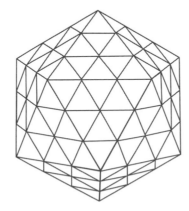

Segmented icosahedron

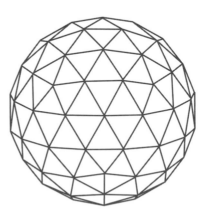

Corresponding sphere

The icosahedron is a platonic body and ideal for the construction of a geodesic dome (a spheric dome with a substructure of triangles). Every corner mark of an icosahedron lies on the surface of a sphere. The adjustment according to the rules of an icosahedron allows for the regular allocation of dimples.

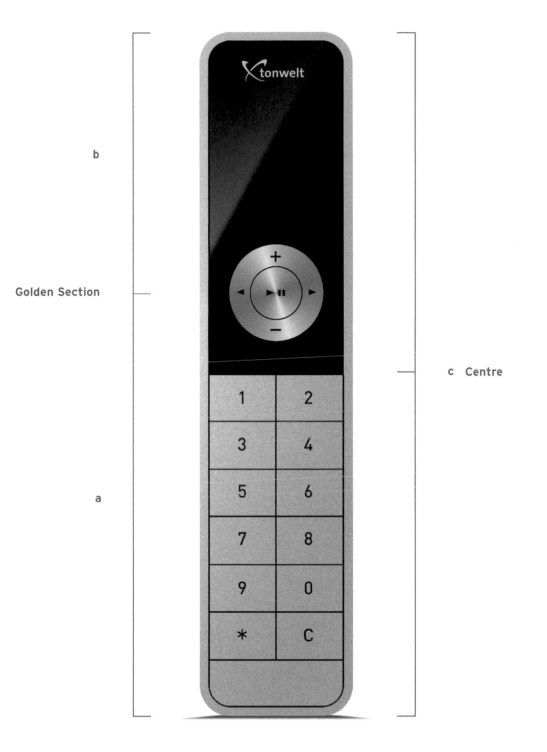

b

Golden Section

c   Centre

a

Audio guide Tonwelt SL Pro
Not only content matters: This audio guide is a companion in museums and exhibitions and should be easy to handle as well as ergonomic.
Tonwelt SL Pro uses a well-known layout and confines itself to the essentials. It radiates calm and clarity. Harmonious and balanced the audio guide
is nonetheless distinctive and unique. (designed on behalf of Tonwelt GmbH)

Reduction

Less is more.
Design elements without any useful function normally have no reason to exist. Unnecessary things distract our brain from the essentials. Needless details often reflect the zeitgeist and can look dated after the event – like pop singer outfits from the 1980's.

In short: Minimalism is the best policy.

Symmetry

Sometimes it is better to do things in halves. With a symmetric design the brain only needs one half of the picture to puzzle the complete one together: A design like this is simpler to grasp. Butterflies, sunflowers, and even human beings are all to a certain point structured symmetrically. The noun "symmetry" describes the ability of geometrical forms to depict themselves on their own. Originating from the Greek word symmetría it means something like harmonious relationships, proportions. Due to its regularity the eye can take in a symmetric form more easily, and that is then more relaxing for the viewer. Symmetry can be created in different ways, in a two dimensional area axial and radial symmetry have to be differentiated.

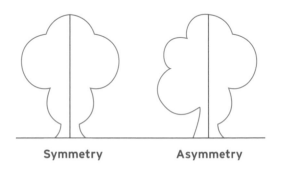

Symmetry   Asymmetry

Axial Symmetry
This variation is also called mirror or reflection symmetry. On a symmetry axis both parts of a form can be mirrored; Both parts are congruent.

Capital letter A for example is symmetrical: If one divides the letter in the middle from top to bottom and folds one part over the other one can see: Both sides of an A are identical.

Radial Symmetry

In nature, flowers are a good example of radial symmetry: Around a point, the so called centre of symmetry, the same forms are mirrored at certain intervals. The petals of flowers are adjusted symmetrically around a centre – providing they have not been removed by someone looking for other answers: "She loves me, she loves me not, she…"

Symmetry creates interesting patterns. Adding forms to symmetrical systems creates a variety of patterns, also called tessellation.

TV-Dongel
The order of venting slots is axis symmetrical.

Asymmetry

Asymmetry, as indicated by its name, is contrary to symmetry; an asymmetrical form cannot mirror itself exactly. An interesting borderline case is the human face. Even though it may seem to be symmetrical at first glance, there are many small divergences on both sides of the face. The perfectly symmetrical face scientists created with a computer program in fact was not more beautiful but far too perfect, sterile and artificial.

In a design process it is a crucial decision at which point forms should be symmetrical and at which point asymmetrical. As is often the case in life there are arguments for both sides. Symmetrical forms are far easier to grasp and understand because humans can perceive the pattern quickly. Asymmetrical forms on the contrary are more interesting in creating diversions. In mechanical constructions asymmetry is sometimes impossible because it would create balance problems. In most cases a good industrial design combines both aspects in a synthesis. The front of a car is symmetric while the sides often enough are asymmetric. Due to varying perspectives symmetry and asymmetry become one entity.

Definiteness

Avoid misunderstandings.
There is nothing like being 'a bit pregnant,' only a yes or no creates clarity. As with the spoken language a design language has to be definite and clear to be understood. Indefinite design forces our brains to work more, we have look more closely to be able to reconstruct the forms in front of our inner eye. Reduced and clear forms we can recognise at first glance and find them pleasant and harmonious.

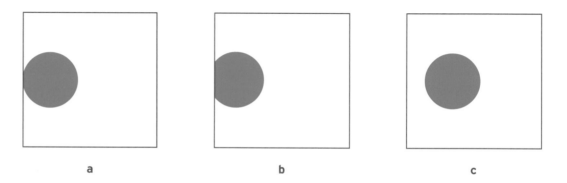

a   b   c

With picture **c** the circle is definitely in the square. In picture **b** it lies clearly at the cut end. Comparing **a** to both **b** and **c** shows that **a** seems more unharmonious because the position of the circle is not explicitly defined.

Regularity

Keep on the ideal line!
When do we like to look a bit longer at an object?
When do we not only want to look at it but crave to touch it with our own hands?

This question can easily be answered with the example of a curve. In short: A curve is an uneven even. In geometry the term curvature describes the change in direction while traversing a curve. But when is this curvature harmonious so that we like to look at it longer? Since our brain likes to reconstruct easily grasped forms, the curvature has to be logical and coherent. A curve is harmonious when it proceeds regularly and does not abruptly change form and direction. Our brain can understand forms better when they have an obvious mathematical background. Therefore, a change in form should be logically comprehensible. The line of a curve, its trajectory is essential in our perception. In mathematics the slope is the measurement of a curve's or line's slant. What does that mean again? Just imagine standing on a road leading up a hill. You want to reach the top so you have to overcome the slope, with every step forward you will move a bit upwards as well. But the steeper the road the more power you will need to move forward. The ratio between change in altitude and the distance covered horizontally defines the road's steepness. This can also be described in mathematical terms:

slope linear function

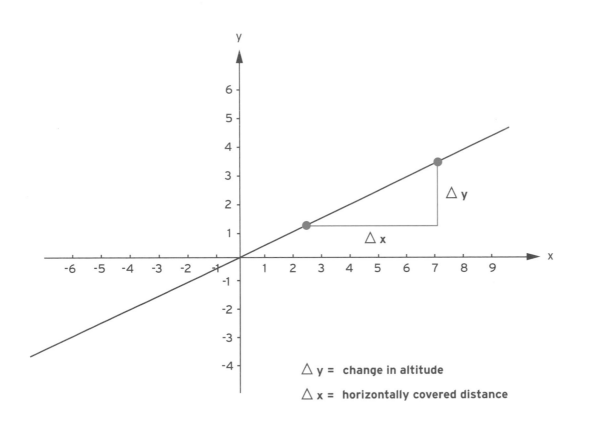

$\triangle$ y = change in altitude

$\triangle$ x = horizontally covered distance

Slope $= \dfrac{\triangle y}{\triangle x}$

The slope is the ratio between horizontal and vertical movement.

If you ask yourself now what the slope of an even has to do with a curve, I have to thank you for your attention. This should simply prove that the slope of an even is constant for the complete length. But this is completely different with a curve; with a curve the slope changes constantly. To stay with this example, imagine once again walking on a road: Sometimes we go up a hill, sometimes down. If the change of slope is regular this seems to be harmonious. Even if you never took an advanced maths course at school, your brain registers the regularity or irregularity of a curved shape. It tries to reconstruct the form and can stomach regular changes far more easily. Complex or irregular slopes are difficult to digest for our brain because they need a lot of time and information to calculate and therefore are unharmonious and unpleasant in the eye of the beholder.

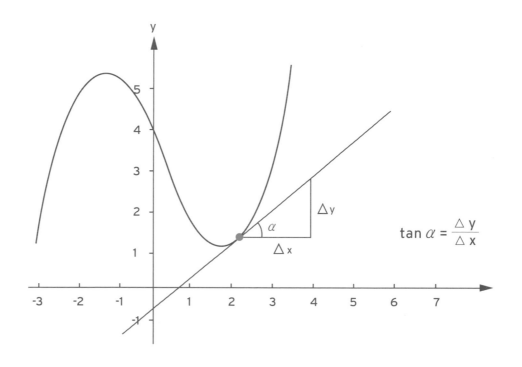

$$\tan \alpha = \dfrac{\triangle y}{\triangle x}$$

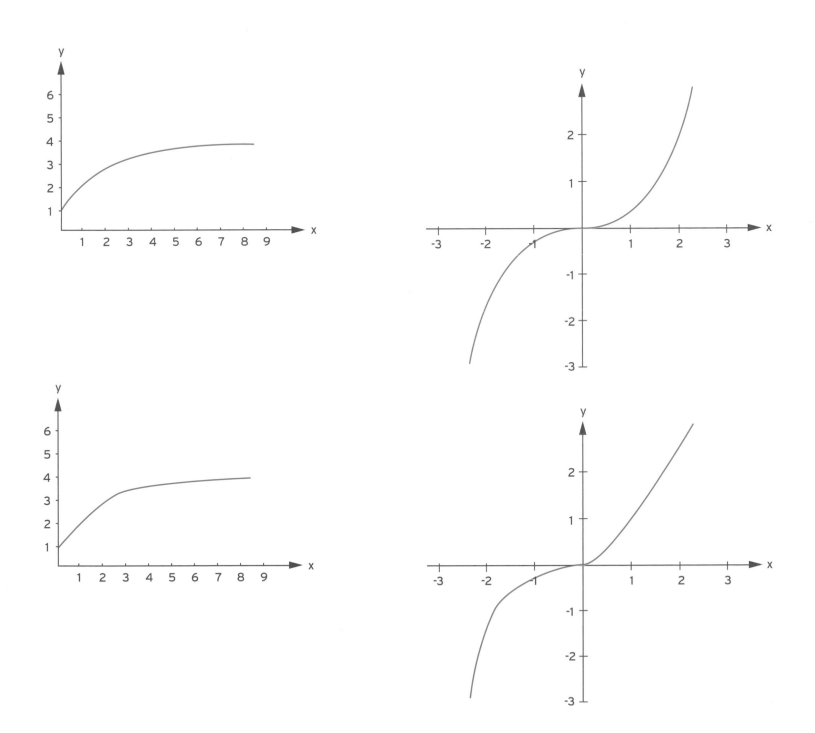

The two images at the top picture show curves with regular slopes. In contrast, the two images below show irregular slopes.

bloomy
The room scent dispenser bloomy seduces. Beauty attracts. The form is that of an opening bud and mirrors the dispenser's function.
The curve formations are regular and smooth creating a harmonious appearance.

Hommage
Stainless steel ball pen with compression mechanics and bent large-capacity lead.

The same principle works for three-dimensional forms. The curvature of a surface in space can be analyzed by studying the surface's curves. It is a way to evaluate the optic and haptic qualities of uneven surfaces which also seem harmonious if their curvature has a certain regularity. But as always: Exceptions prove the rule. Stylistic inconsistency, when used sparingly and sensibly, can purposefully draw attention to a certain feature that is accentuated especially due to this anomaly or irregularity. To put it a bit differently: "It is sometimes necessary to break the rules to make a point!"

Bioaesthetics

Nothing compares to natural beauty.
While bionics primarily studies the technical aspects of nature, bioaesthetics dedicates itself to the aesthetic aspects of nature. Bioaesthetics studies the beauty of natural organisms, their regularity and harmonies – all with the intention of using this insight for developing products. Often enough we have to recognise that we, living on earth, wander through a permanent exhibition of excellent design. And it is not just flowers that serve as a role model for natural aesthetics and design. When taking a closer look we can find extraordinary surprises: The semi-gloss finish and the harmonious curvature of a cockroach's wings can be an inspiration for industrial design. Curving, surface characters, color combinations or the composition and relationship of a natural organism's different components are often enough ideal design templates. 'Beauty' means more than 'beautiful' – there are intersections between bioaesthetics and bionics, and the principle 'form follows function' can be found in nature as well. Harmonious proportions not only look but actually work better. Fish, for example, have a very harmonious form that reduces water resistance while swimming and are therefore often used as a model for the design of ships and submarines. Apart from that, a designer can play with the associations that come with natural forms: The sleek form of a shark was the model for the sports car study that the Corvette Mako Shark was based on. The power, speed and agility the viewer associates with a shark are also perceptible in the car's design.

PowerFlower

Always follow the sun. This miniature solar station recharges electronic devices very efficiently. The faceted sensor in the middle of the station measures the ideal insolation and aligns the station according to that. The principle is based on a sunflower that aligns itself the sun from dawn until dusk. FlowerPower therefore uses the insights of bionics – in addition, the solar station's design recreates the form of a flower and also uses experiences from bioaesthetics.

Higgs (designed on behalf of Fraunhofer Institute for Integrated Circuits IIS)
Always keep an eye open. The mini camera of the Fraunhofer Institute for Integrated Circuits IIS is intelligent, can detect faces and has other features. Experiences made in bioaesthetics acted as model for this form that can especially be seen in the combination with tripod legs. This makes the camera look very active – constantly working and delivering information.

HIGGS
INTELLIGENT CAMERA

Colors

"Color can increase the room temperature by a few degrees."

Colors have a bigger influence than we often think. The moment light hits our eyes it results not only in color perception, but the light spectrum of a color can also trigger certain associations. It is either a result of our personal experiences or presentiments formed and passed on over generations and centuries, anchored in our genes through evolution.

The following short synopsis describes how we receive a certain color and what association it generates.

Red
This color leaves no one cold.
Life, passion and eroticism - all this is united in the color red. But it is as often associated with energy and fire as with fury and aggression. There is a reason we use the term "seeing red" when we are angry.

Blue
A color causes wanderlust.
The color blue first of all seems cool. But in remembrance of a clear blue sky and the width of the sea it is also a color associated with faraway places. Blue reassures and soothes, is clear and dignified. Blue is the color of harmony and gives hope.

Yellow
Looking at this color makes us happy.
Yellow is the color of vitality and joy in life. We know this effect very well, it is the same as the stimulation we get when sunbathing. But yellow stands for the negative feelings of envy and - since it reminds us of gold - greed, too.

Green
This color is quite natural.
Green is the color we meet every day when looking at plants. It is then no wonder that it stands for growth, life, balance and calm. If you get the green light, you get approval to start.

Black
A color that does not really exist.
Vincent van Gogh described black as the "queen of colors," even though from a physicist's perspective black is no color at all. Black surfaces absorb a huge amount of light which make them elegant, classic and exclusive.

White
A symbol for what is good.
In comparison to other colors white (like black) is technically no color at all. Nonetheless white color impressions symbolise purity, light, truth, innocence and perfection.

Silver
The color of modernity.
As a noble metal, silver is always counted as the runner up, second best to gold. But in terms of colors, silver is far better in business. It stands for dynamism, elegance, value and progress.

Gold
The color of splendor.
The sought after noble metal gave the color its name. It is associated with wealth, luxury, and power but also with conservative attitudes and a propensity for extravagance and waste.

Each person has certain colors that fit well with their hair, eyes or skin tone. It is the same with products: Some colors are more favorable to others. Colors shape the character of a product in an essential way: They can for example make it more flashy and noticeable, young, mature, warm, cold, technical, factual, elegant, cheap, classic or futuristic. They can improve the association a certain form intends or create a sharp contrast to it. Even a Ferrari seems tame when painted green instead of Ferrari red.

When choosing a color the place where it will be sold and promoted plays an important role. In Europe, for example, white symbolizes positive characteristics like innocence, cleanliness or wisdom. This is completely different in East Asia or Africa where white is the color of death and grief. A European bride dressed completely in white easily mutates into a grieving widow. Speaking of white: Did you know that bulls cannot actually see the color red? He could not care less if the torero is holding a specifically red cloth in his hand. What really gets to him is the urgent fanning of the cloth, the so-called muleta. In the early days of bullfighting this cloth was white. But because a bullfight is a rather bloody spectacle the cloth was later colored red. That does not make it less problematic but gives the optical illusion of being less bloodthirsty.

Red cloth actually works far better with humans even when it is not being waved around. Red always catches our eyes because it has the highest visible wavelength of electromagnetic radiation. Therefore, it is often used as a signal color, for example on signs, lips or sports cars. A study by the Technical University in Munich proved this: In an experiment they made test subjects listen to the sound of the German express train ICE. On a screen test subjects could see different types of trains passing by. Even though they always heard the same sound and the volume never changed.

But when asked, the test subjects declared the red train had been loudest and fastest of them all.

Another example of the fascinating associative power of colors is the success story of jeans. Jeans are inseparably connected with the color blue. When Levi Strauss moved from Franconia in Germany to San Francisco in 1847, his sole intention was to fabricate robust work clothes for gold diggers. The durable cloth he imported from the French town of Nimes he called 'denim' which meant nothing else but 'from Nimes'. The indigo dye gave it its trademark blue color. The rest is history – the popularity of jeans spread from country to country like wildfire. Whoever wants to give his or her product the appearance of resilience could borrow from the jeans concept. Blue seems extremely wear-resistant and durable – not only because of jeans but because in the early 20th century nearly all work clothing was dyed blue after BASF used a solution to color fabric with synthetic indigo. Dungarees, tunics or aprons – all over the world many work clothes are still colored blue. Associating the color blue with work is the result of a centuries old historical development.

There is another color association that may have been acquired via a painful experience. Be wary of things that are black and yellow - especially when they come in stripes. Whomever an angry wasp has stung might remember why. And there are other dangerous and toxic creatures that use this color combination to discourage potential attackers. No wonder many warning signs take these colors, they caution for example against radioactivity and explosives.

Color Combinations

When working with more than one color it is essential that all the colors fit together. This also counts when different product elements have different colors. Even when offering the same product in various colorings is it necessary to fit all the variations together harmoniously. Because if someone displays different color variations of a product – when they are on sale, for example – the nuances should fit together. In the automotive industry the individual coatings of cars are synchronized and co-ordinated to make sure that when the cars are exhibited together they create a harmonious overall picture. But how to achieve a pleasant color coordination? There is more than one method – which I will discuss in the following sections.

Tone on Tone

Creating a color family

The first step is always to pick a basic color, let us say orange. In the second step one has to create varying nuances of this orange tone that only differentiate in their intensity. The point is to vary the red's quality and lightness. These color families - like human families - bear a striking resemblance to one another. This is important for creating a figurative entity for products. The best results can be reached by varying the nuances in a consistent gradation, therefore avoiding inconsistency in style.

Color Tone

In harmony with a color tone

To create a harmonious series of colors from different color families one can look at the color tone for advice. The term color tone can be defined as a mixture of different colors distinguished by an identical lightness and quality. In contrast to color families one first picks the different colors and then starts to adjust them to each other. One example: The two colors red and blue are very different but can have the same color quality. When choosing a color one can use complementary colors like blue and yellow or choose colors lying next to each other on the color wheel like red and orange. When working with more than two colors it is important to keep the distance between them constant. For that the color hexagon can be of assistance.

Complementary Colors
(from the Latin complementum) is a concept in color theory. In color theory one must distinguish between adding and subtracting from a variety of colors. Opposite colors may also be designated as complementary. When a color is mixed with its complementary color, the result is a neutral gray tone. A pair of colors can also become complementary despite not meeting exact technical and physical industry standards (i.e. RGB, CMYK).

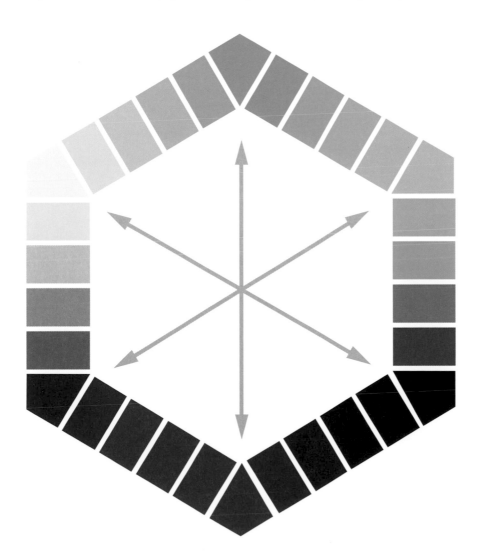

The color hexagon helps with the attribution of colors. It contains the primary colors red, yellow, green, cyan, blue and magenta at its six corners. In between are mixed colors made from colors in the two neighboring corners. The triangles in the inner part of the model show the unique hues red, green and blue but also the other primary colors yellow, cyan and magenta. On the left side the warm colors can be found while the cold colors gather on the right side. Green and magenta form the interface between warm and cold.

Natural Colors

An inexhaustible fountain of inspiration
What is the similarity between an Indian tiger, an Australian coral reef and a German meadow? The creator. All of them were made by nature, and when it comes to colors, nature is anything but mean. Looking for color inspiration one only needs to walk around open-eyed. Strolls through the park, a picnic on a meadow – everywhere there are colors that work quite well together. The usage of colors found in nature leads not only to beautiful combinations, but these colors are perceived as authentic as well – simply because they are the most natural in the world.

A starfish inspired the chosen color tone on the right side.

C 5 | M 0 | Y 90 | K 0
R 252 | G 234 | B 0
Pantone 101 C

C 0 | M 40 | Y 100 | K 0
R 247 | G 166 | B 0
Pantone 130 C

C 0 | M 0 | Y 70 | K 0
R 236 | G 102 | B 2
Pantone 158 C

C 71 | M 100 | Y 0 | K 0
R 109 | G 33 | B 130
Pantone 2612 C

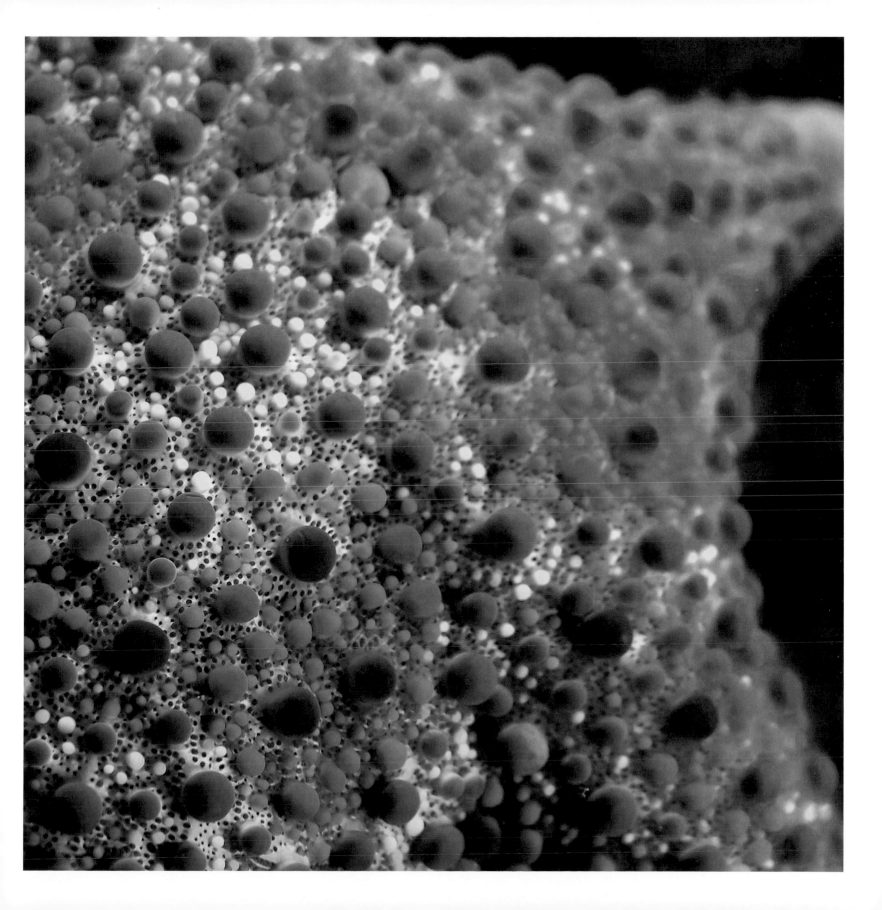

Surface Character and Haptics

"Surfaces imitating other materials are a deception."

How shiny is a material? How does it feel when touched? Both questions play an important role in industrial design. There is a simple procedure to define the surfaces of materials quite easily.

• **Coating with lacquer, colors, rubber painting, etc.**
• **Chemical treatment for example with electrolysis**
• **Physical treatment like polishing, sandblasting, brushing**

To shape surfaces in an aesthetic and haptic way there are two points to consider:

Durability

It is important for a refinement to be long-lasting. One example: A sandblasted surface can have an inhomogeneous shine due to friction and wear. The same goes for electrolyzed refined surfaces that wear down through mechanical abrasion. Every item that is exposed to mechanical strain like screws, tools or gym equipment has to be fabricated well enough to be durable for a very long time.

Authenticity

A surface should not pretend to be something else. Often enough plastic is coated with a metallic coating but one touch tells us what it truly is. The product seems fake and inauthentic. Eventually after the coating has been scraped away and the plastic emerges the once pleasing effect seems cheap and disappointing. Worse still are wood or leather imitations. When using a material one should be confident about the choice and not hide it behind something else.

Optical Illusions

Laying false trails

We cannot always trust our own eyes. And I am not just talking about after that second glass of wine, but every time. The wide field of optical illusions proves that what we think we see and what is actually there are often enough two completely different pairs of shoes. This astounding effect can either lead to an identity crisis or else one could use the effect to make products better. Optical illusions are known from all areas of visual perception. There are for example: Illusions of depth, color illusions, geometrical illusions or movement illusions. How does it work? To put it again more simply: Our brain likes to have prejudices to simplify our life. When reconstructing pictures this leads to a rather basic analysis of the received parameters, in order to put the perceived information into one of the brain's labelled drawers. This principle functions well and makes sense in our everyday life, but the disadvantage is that these prejudices – like in real life – are not always true.

Just take this simple example:

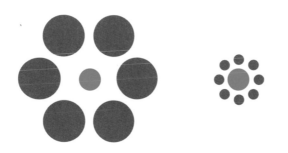

In contrast to other forms we perceive the size differently.

Look at the orange points. Do not cheat: Do you see a difference in size? If you do, you see something that is not actually there. Please feel free to measure and see that both points are exactly the same size. But why do we actually feel that they vary? Parts of our brain's image-processing programs are based on a comparison with other elements. Sizes are not measured only based on exact relations, but in comparison with their surroundings. When looking at the picture on the left the orange point is surrounded with the large grey circles and therefore it seems rather small. In the right-hand illustration it is the other way round.

"Illusions are the usual and not an exception."

Here the grey points are half the size and therefore make the orange circle seem larger. These errors in perception do not only happen in geometry but also with contrasts and colors and even more so with other senses like taste. When eating something sweet first and afterwards something sour, the sour taste is even more overwhelming than usual, a hot drink after a cold one seems even hotter. Pretty average bosses hire even less competent staff to make themselves look better.

Identically colored areas are perceived differently when situated on a color gradient.

Simply look at the stripe in the picture above. Even though it has the same shade of grey on its complete length we perceive an obvious color gradient. But the only existing color gradient in the picture is that of the area below.

What is of most essential importance in industrial design is geometrical illusion. We can play with that, for example, to give an item a slimmer appearance. In the following pictures the black stripe in the middle stands out to catch the eye while the silver areas below and above optically disappear. The external hard drive therefore seems slimmer and as a result (knowingly or unknowingly) becomes associated with product terms like ‚modern,‘ ‚compact,‘ and ‚light.‘

Square
The mobile drive Square fulfils every requirement one might have for a high-quality, mobile hard drive. Due to its curved surface on the top and below it appears rather slim and the high-grade steel platters protect it from scratches. The streak made of synthetic material protects the hard drive from a potential impact if someone drops it.

The Artist's Streak

"Many roads lead to Rome but only one is worth travelling."

Art and design are close relatives, but at the same time they are very different. Industrial design has so many rules and guidelines that completely disagree with the principles of art. Art lives to be free and break rules. Even though there is the Latin dictum: lege artis "according to the rules of art" they do not exist. Art is free while design is not.

This should not sadden the industrial designer: In fact he or she should feel even more encouraged to be creative. The biggest challenge is to use even the smallest stage to escape pragmatism.

Just look at nature again. On the one hand everything is thought through, things function well and complement each other perfectly. It is an incredible overall system. On the other hand we have to be honest: Whoever once designed nature could have been far more pragmatic and boring. An artist's streak even exists in nature.

An interesting and yet most complicated point is that this streak can only be analyzed a little – or not at all. One thing is certain: Every design is also the very personal handprint of a designer. A designer, metaphorically speaking, always puts a part of his soul into the draft. It is this little extra that makes the difference when a customer chooses a product that has the same function as others but is designed slightly differently. People feel and cherish the enthusiasm a designer invests in a product. Even though when asked they often cannot describe in words why they chose one product over another. The artist's streak can be found between the lines.

What is essential for an artistic note:
• **Courage for creative chaos**
• **Joy in positive provocation**
• **Ability to break with conventional thinking**

Playfulness makes a product exceptional and gives it character. It makes it likeable and helps it stick out from the masses Just think about it: We often love other people not despite but because of their rough edges and flaws.

As always: Do not exaggerate! Otherwise art turns into kitsch. Genius and insanity lie famously close together.

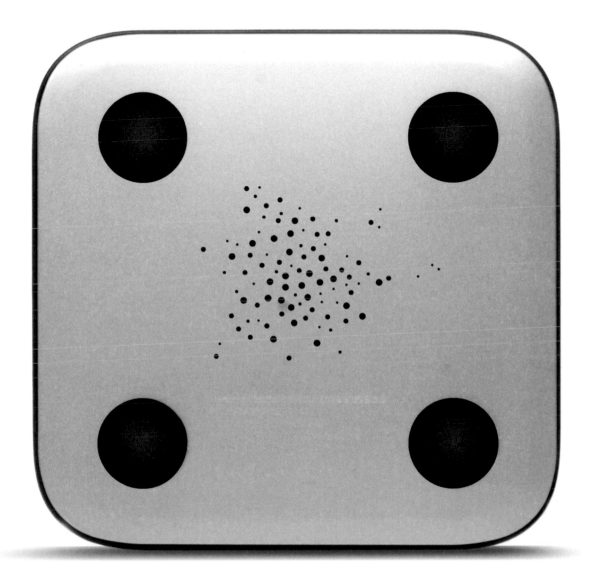

The ventilation holes at the back are not sorted into order but into chaos.

04
MATERIALS

"A DETAILED ANALYSIS OF MATERIAL KNOWLEDGE IS NOT
APPROACHED. IT WOULD BREAK THE MOULD."

Nobody is Perfect

Materials are like humans – they have their strengths and weaknesses. Some are hard others soft, some are flexible, other will not even budge a centimeter. Next to the more classic materials there are new high-tech materials. The topic is far too complex to discuss in full. Therefore, on the following pages I will only describe certain material properties that play an important role in industrial design.

Mechanical Properties

Strength

Being resilient
In simple words: Strength is the ability of a material to withstand external forces without being damaged or irreversibly deformed. While elastic deformations are reversible, plastic deformations are irreversible and the material doesn't return back to its initial state after the force has been removed. The consistency of a material can be measured by how much force is necessary to deform it irreversibly. Depending on the direction of a force, one speaks of tensile, compressive or bending strength.

Tensile strength means a material's ability to withstand tensile force before breaking down.

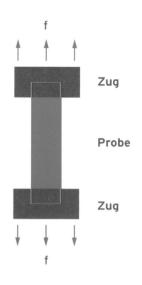

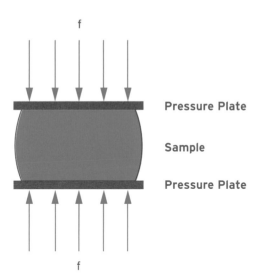

Compressive strength means a material's ability to withstand compression forces before breaking down.

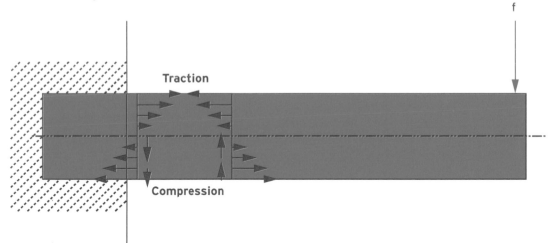

Bending strength is the ability to withstand flexure forces before material failure.

One could think that all three forms of strength and firmness are the same in one material: That tensile, compressive and bending strength all have the same effect and are responded to with the same resistance. But that is not true. One simple example can prove the different effects the direction of acting forces can have on a material. A piece of chalk has a very meagre bending strength. Only a slight bend is enough and - crack! Such a case is called a failure of material. While being bent, chalk traction forces are working on the top and compression on the lower part resulting in the fracture. Chalk cannot resist traction forces and easily breaks down in the upper part. The chalk ruptures and breaks in two. There is no repairing this piece of chalk even if it withstands compression rather well. Have you ever tried to break a piece of chalk only by pressing it with your hands? It is nearly impossible. Chalk is very strong when it comes to compression. To achieve a high level of resistance to bending it is therefore important that the material is able to withstand traction and compression equally. If one of the two components is less highly developed the material becomes easy to break, since bending forces are always a combination of tensile and compressive forces.

Comparable features can be found in concrete – but in bigger dimensions. Concrete cannot resist traction for long. Houses made of cement would not exist had builders not found a way of combining it with steel. At those points where traction forces are at work reinforcing steel is integrated into the structure to protect it. Steel combined with cement has the ultimate tensile strength. This shows that combining different materials often optimizes the result. Both materials compensate for their weaknesses and combine their strengths.

Of course, one has to consider whether both materials also work together on other scales. It is like in a marriage: Not only do the strengths and weaknesses have to be considered but the construction also has to work well in daily life. With cement and steel this is nearly ideal. Steel does have one big weakness: In the short or long term it corrodes. But this is no longer a problem since the alkaline properties of cement prevent any corrosion. Another aspect is that cement and steel have nearly the same warmth specific elongation, which means that when getting warm they stretch nearly in the same way and shrink when it is getting cold. If this were not the case steel cement constructions would be damaged as a result of fluctuating temperatures – houses made of those materials would then be a rather bad idea. But since both like each other and work jointly they make a fruitful marriage in good and bad times.

Hardness

Keeping up appearances.
Hardness and strength sound as if they should mean the same thing. What both material properties have in common is that both are meant to resist forces from the outside. But there are differences between these two. Hardness among other things describes the degree to which a substance withstands wear and tear. Hard glasses and watch glass resist scratches and stay beautiful far longer. There are different testing procedures to examine a material's hardness. The two mostly used and best known are Rockwell and Vickers.

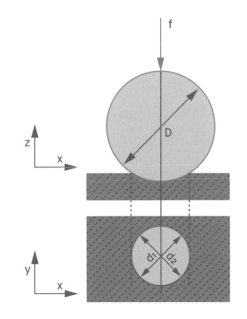

Hardness is the mechanical resistance against a harder material penetrating its surface.

The Rockwell Assay Method

determines the Rockwell hardness of metallic materials. For that an indenter is put upon a material's surface with a certain amount of pressure. The lesser the penetration depth the harder the material. Rockwell Hardness is measured in HR (Hardness after Rockwell).

According to the tested material different indenters are used. This can directly be seen by means of the Rockwell Hardness unit. When for example a cone shaped test probe with a diamond tip is used the unit is called HRC. A Nirosta© stainless steel knife blade has a hardness of about 53 HRC, a gear shaft in comparison has a hardness of "only" 48 HRC. A diamond with 100 HRC is the measure of all things.

The Vickers Assay Method

determines the Vickers Hardness for an amount of materials ranging from aluminium to hard materials like titanium carbide. A pyramid-shaped indenter made of diamond puts a certain pressure upon a material. The remaining imprint is measured under a microscope; the hardness is calculated based upon the imprint-length (d1, d2) of the diagonal. The same indenter is used for soft and hard materials. The hardness is measured in Hardness after Vickers HV. To give two examples: A Japanese Katana sword has a Vickers Hardness of about 600 HV, titanium carbide has a slightly higher scale of 3,200 HV. That makes titanium carbide a valuable material for coating a surface.

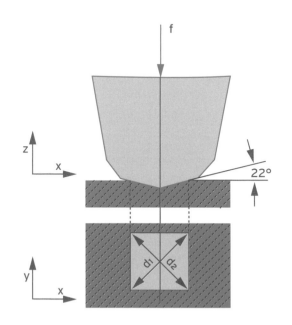

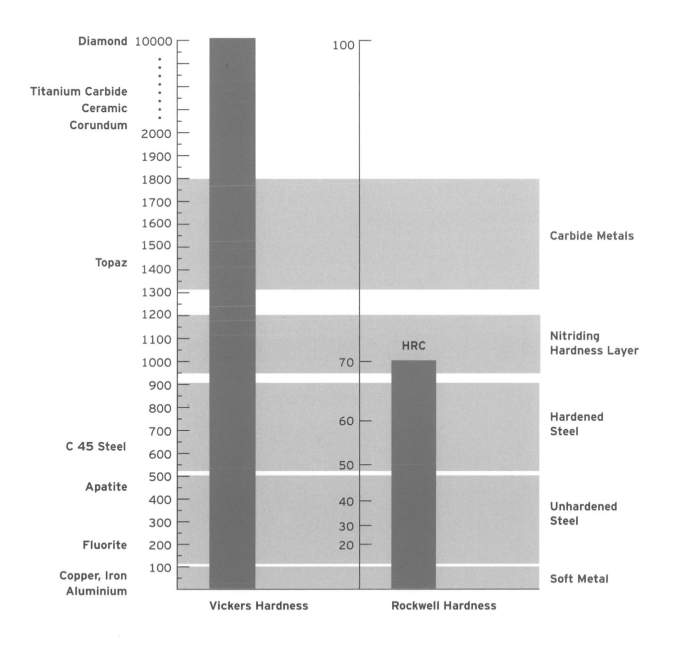

Diamond — 10000

Titanium Carbide
Ceramic
Corundum
2000
1900
1800

Topaz — 1700
1600 — Carbide Metals
1500
1400
1300

1200
1100 — Nitriding
Hardness Layer
1000 — HRC

C 45 Steel — 900
800 — Hardened
700 — Steel
600

Apatite — 500
400 — Unhardened
300 — Steel

Fluorite — 200

Copper, Iron — 100 — Soft Metal
Aluminium

70
60
50
40
30
20

Vickers Hardness   **Rockwell Hardness**

Shore Hardness

Elastomer materials and plastics on average are softer than other materials like metal or minerals. Therefore a far softer method is needed to measure their hardness. In 1915 the US-American Albert Shore developed a new procedure for measuring the hardness of elastomers and rubbery-elastic polymers. His name gave it its title. The device for measuring Shore Hardness consists of a spring-loaded hardened steel pin. The penetration depth (h) into the tested material reveals its hardness. According to the form of the pin and the used spring force procedure Shore **a**, **b**, **c** and d have to be differentiated. Most times tests use Shore **a** or Shore **d**. With Shore **a** the force of 12.5 Newton is used to put pressure on the material, Shore **d** uses 50 Newton. With Shore **a** the steel pin has a flattened tip, with Shore **d** the steel pin has a conical tip. The Shore hardness **a** is used for soft rubber, Shore **d** for harder plastics like elastomers. Since synthetic materials are heavily influenced by temperature, every measurement takes place at a temperature of 23° C +/- 2K. The scale lies between 0 and 100 Shore. The higher the figure the harder the material.

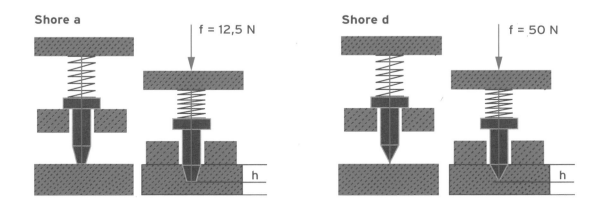

Shore a   f = 12,5 N   **Shore d**   f = 50 N

Method Shore **a** uses a force of 12.5 Newton, Shore **d** uses a force of 50 Newton. The steel pin in Shore **a** has a flattened tip while in Shore **d** the tip is conical.

Material	Shore a
Hardness of Gelatine	0
Gummi Bears	10
Car Tire	50 to 70
Hard Plastic	100

Material	Shore b
ABS	75 to 80
PP	65 to 75
PC	82 to 85
PS	80
PVC-U	75 to 80
PMMA	87 to 88
PE-LD	40 to 50
PE-HD	50 to 70
POM	79 to 82
PA66	80
PA 610	78
PA 612	75 to 80
PA66/GF	85
PP/GF	70 to 75

Neolog A24
The casing was forged from rust-free steel and covered with titanium carbide. Together it builds a surface hardness of approx. 3200 HV

Elasticity

A constant back and forth

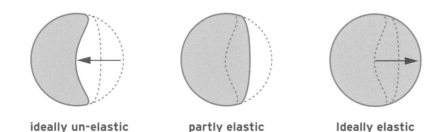

| ideally un-elastic | partly elastic | Ideally elastic |

Elasticity is a material's feature to reversibly react to certain forces being at work.

A metallic scroll spring symbolizes elasticity like nothing else. Under pressure it changes form, but the moment that force ceases the scroll spring turns back to its original form. Elasticity is an important factor in materials. Many elastic materials – like the synthetic material ABS – is used in nearly every product we encounter in our everyday life. A material's elasticity, its ability to compensate small deformations, is used in industrial design for many purposes. Sometimes it can replace mechanic constructions that would be far more expensive and complex, for example the snap lock of a shampoo bottle. Thanks to elasticity the latch can be opened and closed easily. The use of plastic therefore is of value. Another plus point is plastic's ability to deform when confronted with a heavy impact. Through deformation the time frame of the impact is increased as well as the contact surface. This reduces the power spike during a crash and therefore lessens the damage. The effect is not only used for rubber rooms in psychiatric wards but also for many other products.

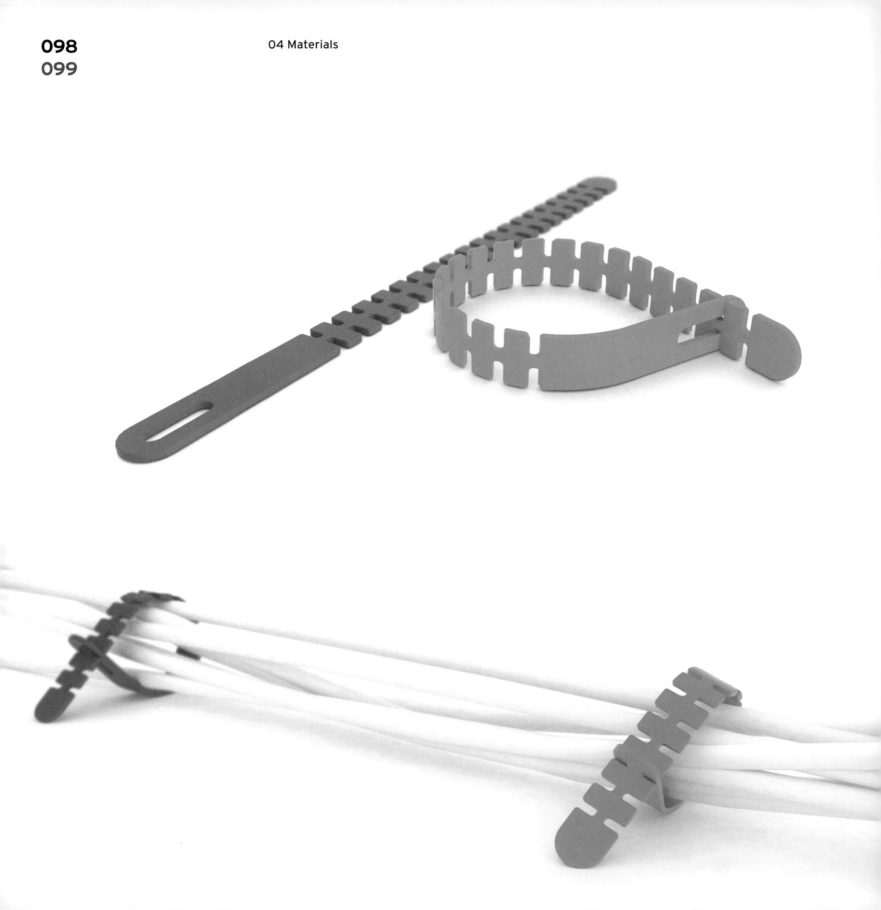

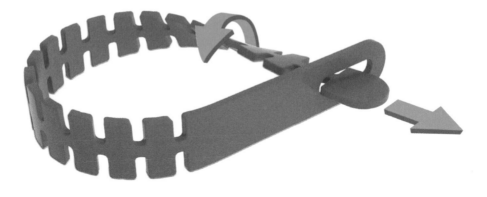

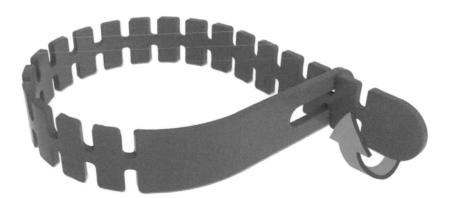

Boneband
The cable tie Boneband takes advantage of the materials properties to replace a complex fastening construction. The material's elasticity guarantees a firm hold and enables the reuse of the tie.

Density

An easy way to stability.

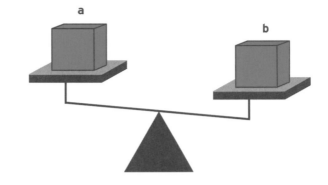

Density describes the relation between a material's mass and its volume.

Material **b** has the same volume as material **a** but weighs more, therefore we can conclude that **b** has a higher density than **a**. Density is an important sign of efficiency, it defines the relation between weight and volume. In many areas materials with a high strength and at the same time minor weight are required. The monocoque of a Formula 1 racer for example has a very stable chassis that can resist speeds up to 200 miles per hour. Its construction consists of a carbon strengthened synthetic material and is not only far more lightweight than the formerly favoured aluminium but also has very special features concerning rigidity.

Often enough the density of a material relies on its use. Density defines how efficient a material is compared to other material properties. Just imagine a bicycle: The frame should be robust and resist tensions. At the same time it should be as light as possible. A bicycle made of Steel 316L would be extraordinarily stable but would weigh a bit too much. Certainly many cyclists would lose interest in using it after a very short time. Modern alternatives are Kevlar and carbon – they offer maximum stability and minimum weight.

Chemical Properties

As with any other substance materials have a lifecycle. They change according to environmental impact like ultraviolet rays, heat, and humidity as much as due to constant stress through vibrations, compression or tractive forces. These can impair function over the long term. Therefore when choosing a material it is important to consider chemical features as well.

The most essential chemical features are:
- **UV resistance**
- **Humidity resistance**
- **Thermostability**
- **Flammability**
- **Translucency**
- **Corrosion resistance**

Let us take wood for an example. Wood is nature's wonder material: solid and workable, naturally degradable, aesthetic, non toxic. But sadly enough it is not perfect and deforms in time. Hygroscopic features are to blame: Wood absorbs the humidity of its surroundings resulting in fluctuation in form due to swelling and shrinkage. The result is that a beautiful wooden table becomes wobbly after a few years use and solid wood windows can no longer be shut properly. Many synthetic materials like PP and APS change as well during time. Plastic cases become brittle and acquire an unhealthy looking yellow tone. That is why plastic is often considered to be something cheap. To prevent changes caused by our natural environment they can be pre-treated. Additives can change the features of synthetic materials. Plasticizer prevents brittleness and hardness, stabilizers increase the lifespan and protect the product from other influences like oxidation and UV light. Even the features of wood can be improved when it is pre-treated, for example with the wood modifier TMT, or in letting it be stacked for a longer time or pre-treating it with UV radiation.

"Every material has it own problematic area."

Material Processing

"A product does not only have to be good but produceable as well."

Besides hardness and elasticity there are other material features essential for a product. Equally important is the possibility to shape it into a desired form in serial production. Only after a material can be handled easily and precisely as a product can it then be fabricated in bigger quantities and for a reasonable price.

Important criteria for material processing are:

Castability
Can a material be made highly fluid and will there be bubbles or cracks after casting?
Will it shrink?

Formability
Can a material be re-shaped durably?
Are procedures like rolling, forging or other possible?

Machinability
Can a material be worked with machining techniques like drilling, turning, milling or cutting?

Composite materials like Kevlar or carbon are good (or bad) examples for how important the processability is when choosing a material. They have a good stability and hardness and are light at the same time. That is why they are used in aeronautics. When in the 1980s these materials were used for the first time for Formula 1 cars, the automotive manufactures could not fabricate the parts themselves. Because of the difficult fabrication process they were produced by the aerospace industry. The fabrications of these high-tech materials were complex and expensive because they had to be fabricated under high temperatures and extremely high pressure in a special furnace.

Ecological Properties

Every product is constantly interacting with the world. Trees have to be cut if you want to build a wooden table. For a plastic computer casing oil has to be dispersed into its particles to get the ingredients needed for the production process. If – after only a few years use – a computer is thrown into the trash this has an impact on nature as well. Energy is needed for recycling which creates new pollutant emissions. Even more bizarre is the export of wealthier nations' waste to poorer countries. The ecological features of a material can help to protect our natural resources and environment. The use of renewable energies is a start. Wooden houses are not only built from a renewable resource but also have excellent features to assure a quality in living. Organic clothes do not only create a good figure but a good conscience as well. It is important that products are made from renewable and regionally produced materials. That reduces transport routes and supports regional business. Sounds too good to be true? Okay, what to do when in order to create a product a designer cannot relinquish a certain material – because of its features, the costs or the client who desperately wants to have it? Even then it is necessary to look more closely, as alternatives exist for special materials as well. Toxic substances should better to be avoided. Many IT manufacturers, for example, have pledged to reduce the use of bromine based flame-retardants in their products. The use of lead today is almost completely forbidden in Germany. These are only two tiny little stones in a big mosaic. A designer can actively protect the environment by thinking a bit further out of the box and not just settling for the status quo.

These factors are essential for ecological features:

Resources
Do the resources exist in large quantities? Or is it necessary to save resources by using alternative materials?

Energy Consumption
How much energy is needed for the fabrication? Are there energy efficient alternatives in materials?

Toxicity
Does a material consist of toxic ingredients or are they superseded by fabrication? Can these substances be replaced by non-toxic material?

Recycling
Can the material be recycled well enough? Does this process require as little effort as possible?

"We should give nature back something better than only waste."

"Together more can be achieved –
that also counts for material."

The magic word is "combination"
An industrial designer has a position similar to that of a soccer trainer: A trainer has to put the right person with the right abilities in the right position. Only then can a team become successful. As much as the football players complete each other, materials in design should be used in a way that allows them to contribute their strengths and compensate for each other's weaknesses.

The mortar Milli is a good example of successful teamwork: Ceramic materials possess an extremely hard surface but are difficult to process precisely. They are also brittle and fragile. Synthetic materials like plastic work the exact opposite way. They lack hardness but can be shaped quite easily. Therefore it is an option to combine both materials when fabricating a mortar in a way that they can rely on each other's strengths. The areas exposed to friction are made from ceramic while the pestle's handle and the bowl's bottom are made from silicon. The silicon parts shield the mortar from damage when accidently dropped and by doing so increase the practical value.

Milli - an intelligent kitchen helper
Milli creates the necessary friction and at the same time maintains as much contact as possible between mortar and pestle so that nothing remains stuck on the sides. The uneven dimples are concave, have a big surface and are not very deep. The dimple's margins are sharpened to heighten the friction. Ceramic is very fragile and is therefore used only at the bottom of the pestle and for the mortar's core areas. All other parts are replaced by silicon.

05

ECONOMIES AND ECOLOGY

"A GREAT SEA IS FORMED FROM MANY SMALL DROPS."

PERSIAN PROVERB

"As children we all learned arithmetic – but why?"

Erich Fried

The Double E

Economy and Ecology are often perceived of as two counterparts. But it has to be considered, if instead there could be two birds killed with one stone: A design so well thought-out that by reducing the amount of materials one could save costs, protect the environment and go easy on natural resources.

Reducing Material Consumption

"When using only one gram too many we already betray nature."

Industrial designers carry a great deal of responsibility. Especially when speaking of high quantities, even small sums can end up as considerable costs. For example, 10 g of unnecessary material in a serial production of 100,000 pieces adds up to a 1 t loss of material. This happens even though there are simple and effective ways to reduce material costs without threatening the longevity and stability of a product.

Ideal Forms

Please imagine you have to design a can for a company that produces canned ravioli. This should have a determined volume, let's say 0.5 litres. And according to the method of production it has to have a cylindrical form. There are unlimited possibilities for realizing this. The can, for example, may be wide and flat or narrow and therefore very high.

All three cylindrical forms in the following graphics have the pre-determined volume of 0.5 l. The form in the middle has the smallest surface and therefore minimal material consumption. Compared to the other alternatives about 20 % less material is needed. Sure, this might only be a few grams for a single can. But with a production volume of about 1 million ravioli cans a year this adds up to a couple of tons every year.

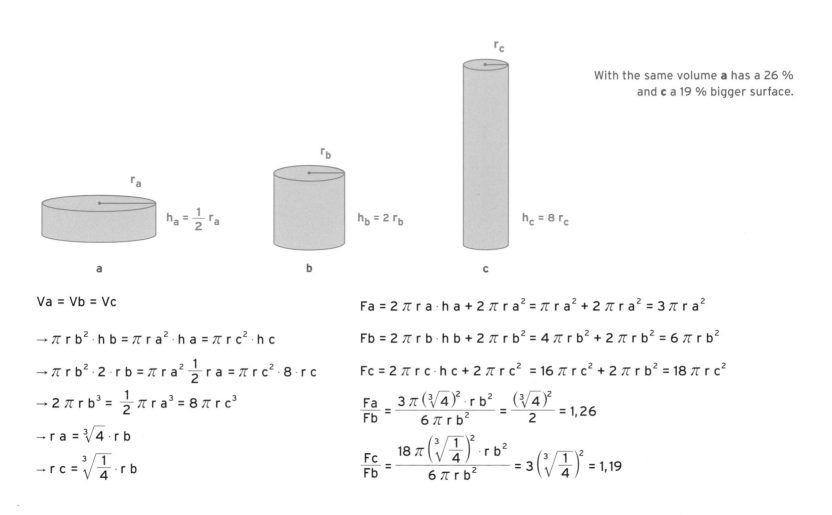

With the same volume **a** has a 26 % and **c** a 19 % bigger surface.

$$V_a = V_b = V_c$$

$$\rightarrow \pi\, r\, b^2 \cdot h\, b = \pi\, r\, a^2 \cdot h\, a = \pi\, r\, c^2 \cdot h\, c$$

$$\rightarrow \pi\, r\, b^2 \cdot 2 \cdot r\, b = \pi\, r\, a^2\, \frac{1}{2}\, r\, a = \pi\, r\, c^2 \cdot 8 \cdot r\, c$$

$$\rightarrow 2\, \pi\, r\, b^3 = \frac{1}{2}\, \pi\, r\, a^3 = 8\, \pi\, r\, c^3$$

$$\rightarrow r\, a = \sqrt[3]{4} \cdot r\, b$$

$$\rightarrow r\, c = \sqrt[3]{\frac{1}{4}} \cdot r\, b$$

$$Fa = 2\, \pi\, r\, a \cdot h\, a + 2\, \pi\, r\, a^2 = \pi\, r\, a^2 + 2\, \pi\, r\, a^2 = 3\, \pi\, r\, a^2$$

$$Fb = 2\, \pi\, r\, b \cdot h\, b + 2\, \pi\, r\, b^2 = 4\, \pi\, r\, b^2 + 2\, \pi\, r\, b^2 = 6\, \pi\, r\, b^2$$

$$Fc = 2\, \pi\, r\, c \cdot h\, c + 2\, \pi\, r\, c^2 = 16\, \pi\, r\, c^2 + 2\, \pi\, r\, b^2 = 18\, \pi\, r\, c^2$$

$$\frac{Fa}{Fb} = \frac{3\, \pi\, \left(\sqrt[3]{4}\right)^2 \cdot r\, b^2}{6\, \pi\, r\, b^2} = \frac{\left(\sqrt[3]{4}\right)^2}{2} = 1{,}26$$

$$\frac{Fc}{Fb} = \frac{18\, \pi\, \left(\sqrt[3]{\frac{1}{4}}\right)^2 \cdot r\, b^2}{6\, \pi\, r\, b^2} = 3\left(\sqrt[3]{\frac{1}{4}}\right)^2 = 1{,}19$$

Naturally we cannot produce every product according to this principle and not all content will be as flexible as ravioli. Nonetheless we can conclude:

For every geometrical form there exists an ideal ratio between surface and volume.

As the best possible constellation, it minimizes material use in order to reach a certain volume. This ideal ratio can be mathematically determined quite easily by calculating the extreme value. The best thing about this is: It can be adapted for nearly all the products and packaging that surround us, for example: Those disposable cups handed out a million times every day in aeroplanes. The perfect form can reduce waste without giving passengers less to drink.

Va = Vb   a   b

$\rightarrow \pi\, r\, b^2 \cdot h\, b = \pi\, r\, a^2 \cdot h\, a$

$\rightarrow \pi\, r\, b^2 \cdot r\, b = 3\, \pi\, r\, a^2 \cdot r\, a$

$\rightarrow r\, b^3 = 3\, r\, a^3 \rightarrow r\, a = \sqrt[3]{\dfrac{1}{3}} \cdot r\, b$

$Fa = 2\, \pi\, r\, a \cdot h\, a + \pi\, r\, a^2 = 6\, \pi\, r\, a^2 + \pi\, r\, a^2 = 7\, \pi\, r\, a^2$

$Fb = 2\, \pi\, r\, b \cdot h\, b + \pi\, r\, b^2 = 2\, \pi\, r\, b^2 + \pi\, r\, b^2 = 3\, \pi\, r\, b^2$

$\rightarrow Fa = 7\, \pi\left(\sqrt[3]{\dfrac{1}{3}}\right)^2 \cdot r\, b^2$

$\rightarrow \dfrac{Fa}{Fb} = \dfrac{7\, \pi\left(\sqrt[3]{\dfrac{1}{3}}\right)^2 \cdot r\, b^2}{3\, \pi\, r\, b^2} = \dfrac{7}{3}\left(\sqrt[3]{\dfrac{1}{3}}\right)^2 = 1{,}122$

Despite having the same volume **b** has 12 % less surface than **a** and needs 12 % less material. Additionally, the form of cup **b** is more stable because the center of gravity lies further down.

On the contrary: The lower and wider the form of the cup, the greater the possibility that the orange juice or cola lands in the passenger's stomach and not their lap. The ideal form is not only resource-efficient but – just as an added bonus – also almost tilt-proof.

And now imagine how big the saving potential could be with bigger products.

The graphic on the following page shows the ideal form for different geometric forms.

Of course the process to finding the right form is far more complex than described below. To find the ideal form there are many other aspects to be considered like ergonomics or legal requirements. And many products are indeed far more complex than a can or a cup. Computers, MP3-players, and tumble dryers for example contain more components that have to be considered in design. To see the principle of the ideal ratio with such products, it is necessary to look at the essential and determined components first. What components cannot be varied in their dimensions? What are the minimum sizes? Are there any ergonomic aspects to consider? If these constants have been found, a rough overall form can be defined that fulfils the specific requirements and has approximately the ideal form with the lowest possible material costs. This should please producers and ecological activists alike.

Surface Area Efficiency (OE)

To show the differences between geometric forms and to get a vivid image of the relation between surface area and volume, it is helpful and necessary to define a new standard to compare different geometric forms. At first glance one can grasp the material costs and a form's resource efficiency. Remember the quote in Chapter 2 about compactness: "The most compact geometrical form is a sphere From a mathematical point of view a sphere has the maximum volume combined with a minimum surface area."

That means the sphere uses the smallest surface area for packing. Therefore we take that as the measure of all things and compare it to other forms. Let us call the ratio between a sphere's volume and surface: 'Surface area efficiency.' The unit surface area efficiency helps to assess how efficiently a geometrical form is designed. The sphere as a model has the maximum value of 1.

	Volume (V)	Surface Area (S)	Ideal Height (h)	V/O	Surface Area Efficiency (OE)
	$V = \dfrac{4\pi r^3}{3}$	$O = 4\pi r^2$	constant	0,207	1
	$V = \pi r^2 h$	$O = 2\pi r^2 + 2\pi r h$	$h = 2r$	0,181	0,87
	$V = \delta a^2 h$	$O = 2\delta a^2 + 8 a h$	$h = (1 + \sqrt{2})\, a$	0,177	0,86
	$V = \beta a^3 h$	$O = 2\beta a^2 + 6 a h$	$h = \sqrt{3}\, a$	0,175	0,85
	$V = \dfrac{\sqrt{25 + 10\sqrt{5}}}{4} a^2 h$	$O = \dfrac{\sqrt{25 + 10\sqrt{5}}}{2} a^2 + 5 a h$	$h = \dfrac{\sqrt{25 + 10\sqrt{5}}}{5} a$	0,172	0,83
	$V = a^2 h$	$O = 2 a^2 + 4 a h$	$h = a$	0,166	0,81
	$V = \dfrac{1}{3} R^2 \pi h$	$O = \pi R \left(R + \sqrt{h^2 + R^2} \right)$	$h = 2\sqrt{2}\, r$	0,164	0,79
	$V = \dfrac{\sqrt{3}\, a^2 h}{4}$	$O = \dfrac{\sqrt{3}\, a^2}{2} + 3 a h$	$h = \dfrac{a}{\sqrt{3}}$	0,153	0,74
	$V = \dfrac{\sqrt{2}}{12} a^3$	$O = \sqrt{3}\, a^2$	constant	0,138	0,67

See appendix pages 140 – 150

The further a geometrical form gets towards the value figure 1, the less surface it has with a constant volume – the further a geometric form gets towards 0 the bigger the surface and the more material is needed to reproduce the volume. The best part in the law of ideal forms: It does not only work in three-dimensional spaces but in 2D spaces as well. One example: If someone wants to fence off a certain space and at the same time use as little fencing as possible there is only one proper solution to their problem – a circle. To fence a quadratic space it would require about 13 % more fencing material. Should we therefore in future create and build round houses and properties? That is not so easy.

A glimpse at fauna might help: Look at the honeybee. 70,000 bees and their queen live in one beehive inside a very small space. And because bees are not only hard working but also economical, they have their antenna efficiently at the front. Bees need days to build only one honeycomb and obviously for them it makes sense to build economically. Now the question remains: Why don't they build rounded honeycombs when a circle has the ideal surface profile? The reason is simple: Circles do not fit seamlessly upon each other, there will always be small gaps. When circles are placed together some spaces will always get left out. According to Plato only three geometrical forms merge together without leaving gaps (triangle, quadrangle and hexagon). Between these three a hexagon has the best ratio of area to circumference. Hexagon formed honeycombs fit together perfectly and need few building materials at the same time. For quadratic shaped honeycombs bees would need ca. 10 % more wax, for triangle shaped ones even 25 %.

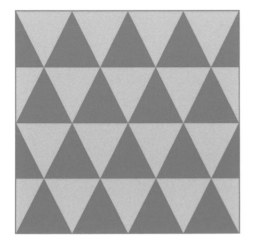

Triangle Grid

Quadratic Grid

Hexagon Grid – also called the honey-comb pattern.

Platonic or regular tessellation of a plane
There are only three possibilities to arrange a regular n-gon tile edge to edge next to each other.

Ideal Statics

The forces and loads acting on a product are the basis in determining the dimensions of its components. Statics defines the necessary material properties, material input and the construction as a whole. Thanks to this a product resists function-related forces and strains.

An intelligent construction helps to reduce material consumption - even if the material properties stay the same. At this point many designers think that the responsibility for costs lies with the engineers, since technicians test every product before actual production starts. If a designer who doesn't know better chooses an inconvenient form, of course an engineer can improve the design so that in the end it lives up to the static requirements. But this solution is a poor compromise; it simply cannot be the ideal. A designer should not base his work on the engineering team's standard right from the beginning, as much as technicians should not suddenly turn themselves into designers. Designers should simply keep static relevant factors in mind right from the beginning. If a technician afterwards tries to turn a donkey into a racehorse, he will never be able to turn it into an Arabian thoroughbred – at best it will become a racedonkey. The ideal form can only be achieved when, from the start, a designer orients the design as a construction that considers function and strains. Otherwise engineers do not only have to readjust, but to change the whole construction. This cannot be a designer's intention and also causes additional work. To find out if a product will resist the strains in practice and over the long term, classic logical thinking is the first step in the design process. Modern proceedings like the finite-element-method (FEM) are a helpful addition in product design. Let us have a look at the topic with a simple example: You are required to design a new clothes hanger. The following questions can be useful: What are the stresses and strains? Which forces have an effect on the hanger? What weight does it have? If we simplify the system as far as possible the distribution of forces looks like this:

The strongest bending moment is at work in the middle of the hanger.

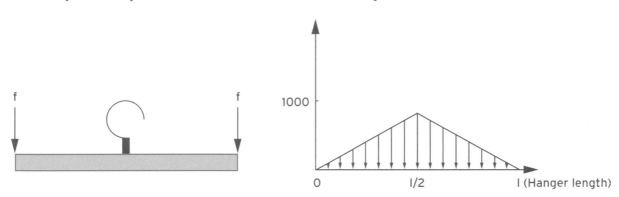

The hanger has to bear the burden of the clothes hung unto it. The types of clothes will be very different – and most likely have a significantly differing weights. Apart from soft and light summer dresses with an approximate shoulder length of 30 to 40 centimeters, there will also be heavy winter coats to carry. To avoid any surprises the designer should always assume the worst-case scenario. If you look more closely at the graphic you can see that the strongest bending moment is at work in the middle of a hanger. If the material lacks enough bending strength at that point the hanger fails: It deforms or even worse – it breaks. Of course a solution could be to use harder materials or a higher material thickness, but apart from that: How can the material input be reduced in finding the ideal form? To depict the impact the design has on the stability more vividly: Please place a plastic ruler above your hands and try to bend the ruler lengthways. This works at best when putting pressure on the flat side. Rotated 90 degrees, however, this looks quite different: It becomes nearly impossible to bend the same ruler that only seconds ago seemed extremely flexible.

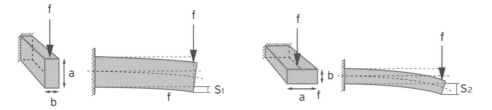

If forces operate on the flat side of a ruler it bends more easily than when the same forces operate on the small side.

This simple example shows what an important role geometry plays in the stability of a product. The same material with the same thickness changes the stability with the direction of the acting forces many times over. Applied to our hanger this means the following:

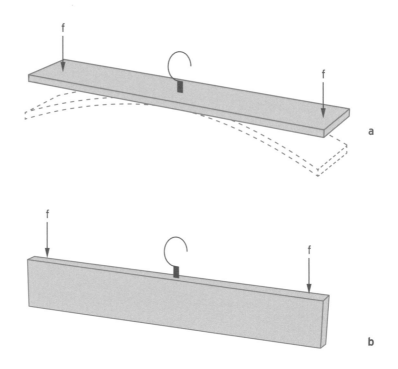

A flat hanger will bend very easily; turned 90 degrees it becomes far more inelastic.

Form **b** would be usable for a hanger but is still not ideal. According to our system the highest strain works on the middle of the hanger. The weight of a heavy winter coat has a special leverage effect in this part. The bending moment decreases towards the outer parts and this creates the potential for saving material. At the hanger's tips the materials usage could be reduced by a fair amount.

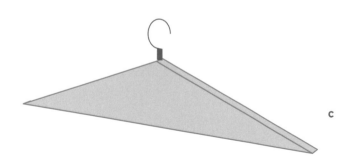

c

The pressure put on the hanger is far less at the outer corners; therefore, the material here can be thinner.

Form **c** gets close to what we describe as ideal form. But still it has disadvantages and could be designed otherwise. It is very stable, needs very few materials and can be produced, for example, from thin sheet metal. But instead broad surfaces at the ends are missing for a better hold on the shoulder areas of a piece of clothing. This would allow for weight to be spread and also protect clothing from damage through hard edges. Let's look again at form a: The form is not very stable but has a flat and wide surface area. So let us combine the advantages of both forms. With just a little twist form a and form c become the nearly ideal form d. The middle of the hanger now has the necessary stability, while the shoulder area now has a wide enough and comfortable surface. Additionally this hanger can be produced easily from very thin material. Even though it has a fine form, the intelligent static allows it to carry even the heavy weight of a winter coat. Another practical effect: The hanger can be stacked and saves a lot of space when transported or stored.

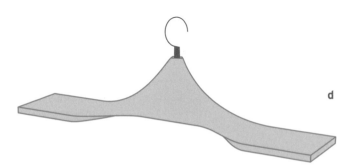

d

Swan
Due to the twist the hanger is very stable and comfortable, the material is used most effectively, form and statics are ideal.

Reducing Production Costs

Time is money, energy too. Not only are the material costs defined by design, the chosen design also determines the manufacturing process and the selection of materials.

Designers have a big impact on how much time and energy is needed for fabricating a product. A thought through design can lessen the amount of CO_2 emissions and reduce the carbon footprint. What kind of process is used depends on the material, the form and the number of units.

Material

Faster shaping into form

An important criterion when choosing a material is the question of how effectively a material can be shaped into a certain form. A material's workability determines, to an important extent, how complex the production will be. Some materials can only be cast while others can only be milled – alternative ones are best shaped into a form through deep-drawing. It is important to know whether the material has to be post-processed afterwards and how many steps are necessary for that.

A good example of how material influences the production process is the newly developed liquid metal. Often searched for but never found, this metal alloy is a "jack of all trades". It combines material properties that for a long time were thought to be incompatible. The American metal specialists Liquidmetal Technologies developed the material that can be cast into every thinkable form without losing its volume when cooling down. This means a long retreatment process is no longer necessary. Liquid metal is also very stable. As well, and thanks to a non-crystallized atomic structure even very tiny and filigree forms are quite resistant. Liquid metal is harder and more elastic than titanium, steel or aluminum and it is extraordinarily light. This new material is often used for military purposes but also in sports equipment like skis or tennis rackets as well as in computers.

Form

Perfect even in the tiniest detail.
Of course there are other relevant factors for choosing a form apart from the production process. But considering the possible techniques can reduce the production costs by a huge amount. It makes sense to determine the requirements of the form in advance and afterwards optimize it according to the demands of production methods. But it is essential that these concessions to economic production are not at the expense of other important factors like ergonomics or aesthetics. As is so often in life there is a proven remedy: Small cause, big effect. Often enough with a minimal change a form can be made suitable for casting, or made so that certain parts can be deep-drawn with relative ease. Even just a rough overview of how the product will work allows the form to be optimized without ruining the look. An ideal form produces less wastage by eliminating potential faults in advance. A product's 'health rate', which describes the ratio between the amount of goods with and without flaws then increases. For example: if only one out of ten products is objectionable one speaks of a health rate of 90 %.

Quantity

Mechanical feasibility
This factor a designer can influence least of all. Most of the time there is actually no alternative to a mechanical production. The most beautiful draft is of no value at all if it cannot be produced in large quantity. This is often evident in the automobile industry. At exhibitions they often show beautiful futuristic models and shapes that later will be seen in the streets in a tamed and easier to produce form. This more or less fine-tuning is a concession to economical producibility. Small quantities have their advantages as well: This gives a designer more space and freedom, as more sophisticated, complicated and extravagant production methods are possible.

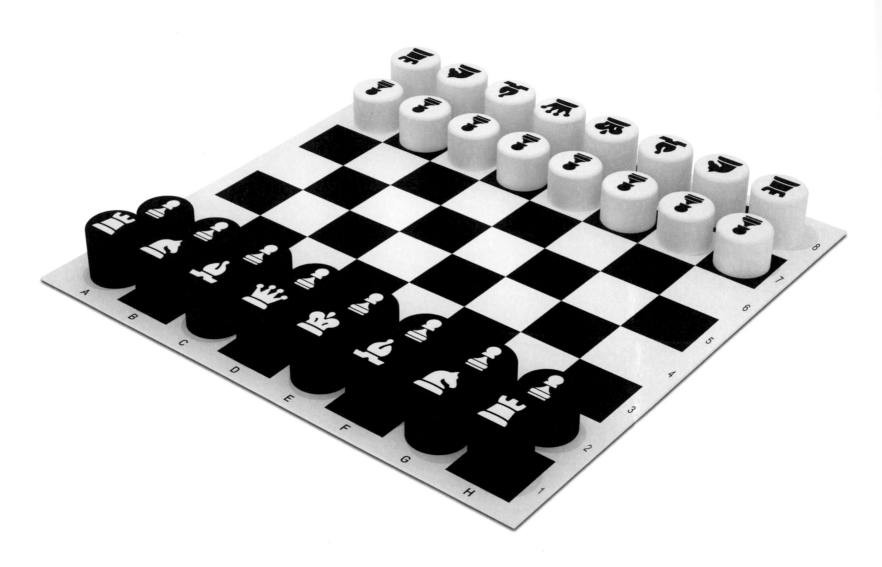

Shah & Shah

The typical graphic depiction of a chessboard is well known from chess books or magazines. They are mostly small pictograms symbolizing the different figures and have become ubiquitous and for chess players are very familiar. Reduced to their essence the pictograms enable the viewer to grasp a scene and get an overview of the complete chess board and scenario. A new design concept takes over this minimalistic reduction and shows a chess board without distracting details. The simple and consistent chess pieces generate calm and harmony and also reduce production costs. They are also easy to clean: Instead of a wooden chessboard a soft silicon pad is used that can be easily rolled up and stored in a cylindrical package.

Reducing the Set-up Costs

For every new step in the production process the machines have to be set-up again. Everything grinds to a halt, nothing can be produced. The design, next to the manufacturing method, determines how complex and complicated it is to adjust the tools and instruments needed for the production. Three golden rules help to reduce the costs for the mechanical set-up:

- **Clarity:** A simple form can normally be produced far more easily.
- **Reduction:** Fewer components reduce the set-up costs.
- **Uniformity:** Uniform elements result in having to adjust a machine only once.

How to reduce the set-up costs of a product can be seen in the design of the chessboard Shah & Shah. Everyone accustomed to the board game knows its typical surface. The graphic illustrations symbolizing the chess pieces are well known from chess books and have been memorized over the years. With the chessboard Shah & Shah the figures' characters are reduced to their essentials: As pictograms on cylindrical bodies. Players have – even more than with a traditional layout – a complete overview. The simple and concentrated forms do not distract, they help draw the focus to the actual play. And they save production costs. The simplified form language only needs two instead of six moulds for queen, castle, knight, bishop and pawn. That reduces the set-up costs by about 66 %. The chessboard is no board at all but a silicon pad that can be rolled up easily and stored in cylindrical packing. Compared with traditional chess games containing hinges and a small locking mechanism, the new design reduces the production costs. And the enjoyable side effect: Due to its unconventional form it stands out among the masses – a unique characteristic that should please both marketing and sales staff.

> "Every additional step results in higher costs."

Reducing Assembly Costs

Optimizing production costs often goes hand in hand with the principles of good design. One of them is that design should never use too many different forms. And this also plays an important role in reducing assembly costs. An efficiently producible product can be a practical outgrowth of professional design. Here is a small example: A new MP3 player has to be designed. It's not only from the aesthetic point of view that having several push buttons with different sizes makes no sense. More buttons unnecessarily increase production costs because different moulds are necessary, and cause additional assembly steps.

> "Good design is most likely also easy to produce."

It is far more efficient to concentrate on creating a few elements that can fulfill the desired functions via smart linkages. When using Jog Dials, for example, only one mould and one assembly step are necessary. All the functions of the player can be managed by the turn of a wheel.

Sustainability and Obsolescence

"Recycling is good, producing less waste even better."

When someone says that today we produce far too much waste this someone is right. Sadly, in more than one way. Firstly, there are many cheap products overfilling the shop shelves that nobody actually needs. Often enough their design costs are non-existent. Secondly: There are a lot of products that become waste after a short timespan – they suddenly no longer function. Products refuse to work, often enough not only because some parts are worn out but because this effect is intended. This is called planned obsolescence. Presumably, if the achievements of the modern age had already existed in Ancient Rome the Colosseum would have long since tumbled down leaving a space for someone to build a new one. This has absolutely nothing to do with sustainability.

Obsolescence means a product becomes out-dated. This can happen as a natural process or artificially. There are different kinds of obsolescence, here are the most important ones:

Planned Obsolescence

This kind of obsolescence is often part of a marketing strategy. Even during construction weak points are predetermined to make a product's lifespan, "manageable", to make sure that the customer has to buy a new product after a short time. Wear and tear is also taken into account to arouse the customer's wish for a new flawless product.

Functional Obsolescence

Should a product no longer be used because of current requirements, one speaks of functional obsolescence. For example, computer operating systems can become obsolete if a new and desperately needed software will not work impeccably with it. The same can happen to printers when there are no longer printer cartridges.

Psychological Obsolescence

With this kind of obsolescence a still impeccably working product nonetheless becomes outdated in the eyes of the customer, as it no longer corresponds to a certain zeitgeist. It is no longer up-to-date. This phenomenon can especially be observed in constantly changing fashion trends. Technical development causes psychological obsolescence as well, for example when analogue photography was replaced by digital photography. Or let us take a look at mobile phones: The knowledge that today's news is tomorrow's old hat can be applied to mobile phone technology. Even though the older device might function properly, many people buy a new phone believing that an up-to-date model is better.

Obsolete Obsolescence

Even though the planned use of obsolescence might improve sales, business growth should never be the base of good design. Here one thing should always be made sure of: Quality over quantity.

Although we are able to recycle many materials, this nonetheless uses lots of energy that could be put to better use elsewhere. And not all material is recyclable as can be seen with so-called rare metals. These substances are not only rare – as their name implies – but mostly cannot be recycled at all. Among the rare metals are molybdenum, niobium and indium. They are essential for many processes, and if they are missing complete production flows can be brought to a halt. Innovative sectors in particular are in need of rare metals that are used for fuel cells, computers, hybrid cars or photovoltaic cells.

The best solution therefore remains: Produce less waste.

Back in the day a man used his razor all his life: He fostered and treasured it with love and passion and then passed it on to the next generation. The new trend of using disposable products that started in the 1950s was also the birth of the plastic one-way razor, colorful and sold 20 in a package. Of course, nobody wants to turn back time so that before every shave a man has to sharpen a razor blade for at least ten minutes. Finding the middle ground between both extremes is the sensible thing to do. The way forward does not lie with ‚disposables.‘ Planned obsolescence is an insane idea and should be banished in business in the years to come. It was never up-to-date and never will be. The ruthless urge to enhance sales figures no matter what the cost not only burdens the environment but also weakens the customer's trust in the brand.

What might seem to be an economic success can become a boomerang returning to its sender, resulting in financial losses and at worse the end of a brand.

The ecological awareness of consumers and societies is constantly growing. The times of fastfood mentality are slowly but surely drawing to an end. Independent watchdog groups and consumer organizations as well as the internet make the quality of products far more transparent. Companies only trying to make fast money on the backs of the environment and consumers will no longer have any chance on the market in the long term. At least this is what we would wish. Warner Philips, grandson of the Philips electronic concern founder, gave a positive signal. Together with the Lemnis company he developed a new LED light that has a lifespan 25 times longer than a traditional light bulb – and thereby is 90 % more efficient. This is even more important when seen in the context of 1924 when the so called Phoebus cartel, an association of international light bulb fabricators, decided to restrict a bulb's burning time to 1,000 hours even though a longer burning time was technically possible. There were regular tests to make sure these restrictions were observed. Cartel members whose light bulbs burned longer than 1,000 hours were sanctioned with severe penalties. Even though the cartel was officially liquidated in 1941 the idea became more popular than one would care for.

But back to more positive things:
To design long-life products one has to observe their function over the long-term. Only continuous stress tests will show a product's weak point. A mattress has to provide reliable stability and comfort not only once but thousands of times. A team of test sleepers is not even necessary for that: It can be simulated equally well with a computer or tested with machines placing pressure on the mattress. When the weak spots are found they can be remedied by optimizing the construction or the material. In general, high quality materials will affirm a customer's choice and strengthen his or her trust in a brand. Another possibility to make a product last longer is to make sure the wearing parts can be replaced. No one thinks his new

car is fit only for the junkyard when just the brake pads have to be exchanged. What might sound self-evident at this point is actually non-existent for many products. For example, the rechargeable batteries of many products cannot be replaced, therefore making it necessary to buy a new device only because this small part is defective. In conclusion we can say there are three possibilities to improve a product's longevity:

- **Adjusting the construction to its strains**
- **Using high quality and durable materials**
- **Replacing parts that typically wear out**

or, better said: Let's dispose with disposables.

MARKETING

"INDUSTRIAL DESIGN IS A COMPANY'S MOST
IMPORTANT BUSINESS CARD."

A Family Affair

Industrial design is never stand-alone. It also always represents the brand and the company for which the product was designed. It is an essential element of corporate design. Even though every model has its specific demands and target group, it should always be recognizable to which family it belongs.

The Importance of Identity

Usually companies and brands are perceived of as people. As with real life, we find some more likeable and pleasant than others. There are for example youthful, highly serious, flipped out, and sportive companies among various others that according to their identity appeal to a certain group. The different characteristics are summarized in a company's corporate identity, known as: CI.

People can be recognized by their looks, their gestures and facial expressions, their origins or language; companies use similar features to be recognizable and distinct. Rivals never rest, making it even more important for a company to differentiate itself from its competitors. The entirety of its communication, visual appearance and every action it takes defines its identity.

The corporate identity defines a company's character. Essential elements are a corporate design, corporate behavior, corporate language and the complete field of corporate communication.

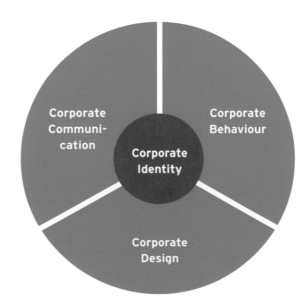

The visual appearance of the CI is determined through the Corporate Design, often shortened to CD. CD determines the mandatory requirements like the logo, corporate colors, corporate fonts, which metaphorical language is used or how working clothes are fashioned. Even the sound design is regulated in the CD, for example which sounds are used in combination with a logo.

Often enough there is a big gap where parts of the Corporate Design should be. One would assume that companies would regard industrial design as a key part of their CD. But far from it: Products may be designed in a more or less sophisticated manner, but often enough there is no consistent line subsequently connecting the various products of the company. Many companies could therefore be diagnosed with a split personality, being one thing in their identity but expressing something completely different in their product's design.

Only slowly have more and more modern companies recognized that industrial design is an essential part of a company's business strategy. A favorable recognizability of products is essential – every item essentially determines a company's image.

To make this a little bit clearer. Just imagine all of a company's products are standing in front of you. They are easy to spot but the logo is concealed. Only if the products resemble each other will you be able to recognise them as being part of one product family, only then can one speak of a defined corporate design. If the design of various products is too diverse, it has the same effect as a cuckoo's egg: It will not really fit into the nest, irrespective of the product family.

At this point it is necessary to also speak about OEM items. Products fabricated by an Original Equipment Manufacturer most often come into the market under a foreign name. An OEM fabricates products and offers them to other companies for distribution. Even though these OEM products might have a company's logo, they do not fit into the firm-specific identity.

A consequent and independent industrial design would have incredible potential to differentiate itself from competitors. Especially since many products today resemble each other more than ever before.

Sphere
Nature was the model for this innovative washing machine. An organic curvature is used to stage the outward appearance and also gets closer to its internal function. A sphere sticks out from the masses, is recognizable and distinctive.

The Definition of a CD

To develop a design resemblance and uniformity for a company's complete range of products is not an easy task. But the effort is worthwhile, especially when a form language is found that can be used on a long-term basis. A customer can recognise the product at first glance as it stands out from the masses. In the best case scenario a new image is created and the brand is made unique.

How to create a sign language for a certain brand?

Repetition

Establishing typical characteristics.
Whether it is the defined curving of edges or a very specific form for control elements: In defining a typical sign language one can also define independent features that when repeated in good proportion with different products of the same firm can create a value of brand recognition. A simple form can also create this unique characteristic: One has only to think of that triangular Swiss chocolate everyone recognizes at first sight.

Equivalence

A consistent overall image.
Similarly used materials can symbolise affiliation with a brand. For example the way a material's surface is treated, the combination of different materials – in professional industrial design this should manifest itself in every product as well. Only that way will all items, like a puzzle, fit together into a big, coherent overall picture. A consistent coloring, a typical finishing of surfaces or the use of typography heightens the affect of family resemblance. Just think of the famous Mercedes Silver Arrow, its typical silver surface unites a wide range of rather different race cars and marks them nonetheless as Mercedes-Benz. On the contrary, when speaking about a red racing car one might mean a racer from Stuttgart. Most people, though, will more than likely think of a famous car from Italy.

Character

A product personality.
Products, like companies, emit a certain character. There are serious, humorous, aggressive, boring, nice, sweet or simply pragmatic products. This results from the fact that certain forms, colors, and materials in our perception provoke different associations. For example, round forms combined with soft materials and vibrant colors appear friendlier than sharp and edgy contours paired with hard materials and a greyish coloring. There is a reason why in movies the bad guys often wear dark garb and carry around a bunch of sharp weapons. We have learned through experience that sharp edges bear a risk of injuries and therefore react to them with a certain respect. Skillfully applied, this learned sign language can be used to give a product a unique characteristic. Thus the created product identity should always be in harmony with a company's identity and never contradict the product's function. Industrial design should not only reflect a product's requirements but also that of the brand. To ideally emphasise the character of a product three points have to always be taken into consideration: The function, the CI and the target group.

A Product's Character in Harmony with its Function

To put it more simply: A product should radiate its function and the appropriate associations. A waterproof device should not only be waterproof but also look 'waterproof.' A sports car should not only drive fast but look fast when parked. We perceive a product's quality optically – if the design is not optimal in this area, a product can have the best quality, but we will not see it. The result: We turn towards a better-designed product without even testing the other one even once. The kitchen knife Sharko is a good example of how optic and function go hand in hand and complement each other. The inspired form resembles a shark. This elegant hunter is known for its knife-sharp teeth. Therefore the dynamically curved shark-like knife form also arouses the association "sharp". Even though this is not a conscious process the spectator cannot evade this effect: The knife seems sharp without even being tested.

A Product's Character in Harmony with the CI

In addition to function the character of a product can also symbolise and strengthen the image profile of the company and brand. The definition certainly depends on the marketing strategy which has been prepared in advance. Not only should the product be well-adjusted to a corporate identity but the product design as well. A product might be best sold to a certain target group through the use of humour, while another target group might be discouraged by such efforts. The best case is an effective entity where a product's design is efficient and fits well into the firm's identity. This makes every product a brand statement.

A Product's Character in Harmony with the Target Group

The question for whom a product is made is essential for market success and consequently relevant in industrial design. Therefore it makes sense to analyze the target group first. Who is the main target group? What characteristics does it have? What interests, expectations and possible dislikes does the group have? Potential customers have to be analyzed to successfully adjust product characteristics according to the target group's needs and wishes.

Two main attributes have to be taken into consideration:
• **Socio-demographic attributes** (gender, age, civil status, income, level of education, cultural roots, etc.)
• **Psychographic attributes** (political attitudes, gender identity, attitude to life, religion, etc.)

Only if we have, like criminologists or profilers, drawn up a comprehensive target group profile, can we assume what a consumer expects and which features correspond with his or her tastes and needs. One would presumably use other colors for the design of a hearing instrument for seniors compared to that of toys for children between the ages of 5 to 8. The real challenge is to put oneself in the position of someone in a target group and try to see a product from their point of view. Narcissistic love for one's own taste, ignorance of a target group's choices and trying always to push through a personal style is unlikely to lead to market success.

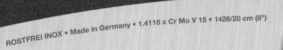

Sharko
The kitchen knife is forged from special blade steel and has a Corian handle. This acrylic bound mineral material distinguishes itself through longevity. The knife's layout is graceful and distinctive. It is no coincidence that the form evokes a shark's streamlined body. This emphasizes the product's sharpness. Indeed, the functionality delivers what the design promises: The knife is designed to make handling most comfortable and ergonomic.

APPENDICES

07

Cone

Objective Function.:

$$F = \pi R^2 + \pi R S = \pi R (R + S) = \pi R \left(R + \sqrt{h^2 + R^2}\right)$$

N.B.:

$$\frac{1}{3} R^2 \pi h = V$$

$$\longrightarrow h = \frac{3 V}{\pi R^2}$$

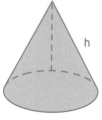

therefore $F = \pi \left(R^2 + R \sqrt{\dfrac{9 V^2}{\pi^2 R^4} + R^2} \right) = \pi \left(R^2 \sqrt{\dfrac{9 V^2}{\pi^2 R^2} + R^4} \right)$

$$F' = \pi \left(2 R + \left(\frac{-2 \times 9 V^2}{\pi^2 R^3} + 4 R^3 \right) \cdot \frac{1}{2 \cdot \sqrt{\dfrac{9 V^2}{\pi^2 R^2} + R^4}} \right)$$

$$F' = \pi \left(2 R + \left(\frac{-9 V^2}{\pi^2 R^3} + 2 R^3 \right) \cdot \frac{1}{\sqrt{\dfrac{9 V^2}{\pi^2 R^2} + R^4}} \right)$$

$$F' = 0 \implies 2 R = \frac{\dfrac{9 V^2}{\pi^2 R^3} - 2 R^3}{\sqrt{\dfrac{9 V^2}{\pi^2 R^2} + R^4}}$$

$$\implies 4 R^2 = \left(\frac{9 V^2}{\pi^2 R^2} + R^4 \right) = \left(\frac{9 V^2}{\pi^2 R^3} - 2R^3 \right)^2$$

$$\implies 4 = \left(\frac{9 V^2}{\pi^2} + R^6 \right) = \frac{81 V^4}{\pi^4 R^6} - \frac{36 V^2 R^3}{\pi^2 R^3} + 4 R^6$$

$$\implies \frac{36 V^2}{\pi^2} + 4 R^6 - 4 R^6 + \frac{36 V^2}{\pi^2} = \frac{81 V^4}{\pi^4 R^6}$$

$$\implies \frac{72 V^2}{\pi^2} = \frac{81 V^4}{\pi^4 R^6} \implies R^6 = \frac{\pi^2 \cdot 81 V^4}{\pi^4 \cdot 72 V^2} = \frac{9}{8} \frac{V^2}{\pi^2}$$

$$\implies \frac{\sqrt{2}}{2} \cdot \left(\frac{3 V}{\pi} \right)^{\frac{1}{3}} = R = \left(\frac{9}{8} \left(\frac{V}{\pi} \right)^2 \right)^{\frac{1}{6}} = \left(\frac{9}{8} \right)^{\frac{1}{6}} \cdot \left(\frac{V}{\pi} \right)^{\frac{1}{3}}$$

and $h = \dfrac{3 V}{\pi R^2} = \dfrac{3 V}{\pi} \cdot \dfrac{1}{\left(\dfrac{9}{8} \dfrac{V^2}{\pi^2} \right)^{\frac{1}{3}}} = \dfrac{3 V}{\pi} \cdot \left(\dfrac{9}{8} \right)^{-\frac{1}{3}} \cdot \left(\dfrac{V}{\pi} \right)^{-\frac{2}{3}} = \dfrac{3 \cdot 3^{-\frac{2}{3}}}{2^{-1}} \cdot \left(\dfrac{V}{\pi} \right)^{1-\frac{2}{3}}$

$$h = 2,3^{\frac{1}{3}} \cdot \left(\frac{V}{\pi}\right)^{\frac{1}{3}} = 2 \cdot \sqrt[3]{\frac{3\,V}{\pi}}$$

Define $x = \dfrac{R}{h} = \left(\dfrac{9}{8}\right)^{\frac{1}{6}} \cdot \left(\dfrac{V}{\pi}\right)^{\frac{1}{3}} \cdot 2^{-1} \left(\dfrac{3\,V}{\pi}\right)^{-\frac{1}{3}} = \dfrac{1}{2} \cdot \dfrac{3^{\frac{1}{3}}}{\sqrt{2}} \cdot 3^{-\frac{1}{3}} = \dfrac{1}{2\sqrt{2}} = \dfrac{\sqrt{2}}{4}$

Objective Function.: $\quad F = 2\,\pi\,R\,h + \pi\,k\,R^2 + \pi\,R^2$

N.B.: $\qquad\qquad \pi\,R^2\,h = V \longrightarrow h = \dfrac{V}{\pi\,R^2}$

$$F = \frac{2\,\pi\,V}{\pi\,R} + \pi\,(k\,R^2 + R^2)$$

$$= \frac{2\,V}{R} + \pi\,(k\,R^2 + R^2)$$

$$F' = -\frac{2\,V}{R^2} + \pi\,(2\,k\,R + 2\,R)$$

$$F' = 0 \implies \frac{2\,V}{R^2} = 2\,\pi\,(k\,R + R) \implies \frac{V}{\pi} = R^2\,(k\,R + R) \implies \frac{V}{\pi} = R^3\,(1+k) \implies R^3 = \frac{V}{\pi\,(1+k)}$$

therefore $R = \left(\dfrac{V}{\pi\,(1+k)}\right)^{\frac{1}{3}}$

and $h = \dfrac{V}{\pi} \cdot R^{-2} = \dfrac{V}{\pi} \cdot \left(\dfrac{V}{\pi}\right)^{-\frac{2}{3}} \cdot \left(\dfrac{1}{1+k}\right)^{-\frac{2}{3}} = \left(\dfrac{V}{\pi}\right)^{\frac{1}{3}} \cdot \left(\dfrac{1}{1+k}\right)^{-\frac{2}{3}}$

Ratio: $\qquad \dfrac{R}{h} = \dfrac{\left(\dfrac{V}{\pi}\right)^{\frac{1}{3}} \cdot \left(\dfrac{1}{1+k}\right)^{\frac{1}{3}}}{\left(\dfrac{V}{\pi}\right)^{\frac{1}{3}} \left(\dfrac{1}{1+k}\right)^{-\frac{2}{3}}} = \left(\dfrac{1}{1+k}\right)^{\frac{1}{3}+\frac{2}{3}} = \dfrac{1}{1+k}$

$$R = \left(\frac{V}{\pi}\right)^{\frac{1}{3}} \left(\frac{1}{1+k}\right)^{\frac{1}{3}} \quad \text{is the minimum.}$$

Compactness of a Sphere

Volume: $V = \dfrac{4\,\pi\,r^3}{3}$

Surface area: $O = 4\pi r^2$

Define compactness (ratio of volume to surface area) $k = \dfrac{V}{O} = \dfrac{4\,\pi\,r^3}{12\,\pi\,r^2} = \dfrac{r}{3}$

for the reference volume $V = 1 = \dfrac{4\,\pi\,r^3}{3}$

we obtain $r = \sqrt[3]{\dfrac{3}{4\,\pi}}$

Therefore the compactness of a sphere will be: $k = \dfrac{1}{3}\sqrt[3]{\dfrac{3}{4\,\pi}} \approx 0{,}2068$

Therefore the compactness of a sphere is now used as a reference to calculate a body's grade of compactness.

Define grade of compactness $\gamma = \dfrac{k_{\text{Solid Figure}}}{k_{\text{Sphere}}}$

Tetrahedron

Volume: $V = \dfrac{\sqrt{2}}{12}\,a^3$

Surface area: $O = \sqrt{3}\,a^2$

Therefore we obtain the tetrahedron's compactness: $k_T = \dfrac{V}{O} = \dfrac{a\,\sqrt{2}}{12\,\sqrt{3}} = \sqrt{\dfrac{2}{3}}\,\dfrac{a}{12}$

For a certain reference volume $V = 1 = \dfrac{\sqrt{2}}{12}\,a^3$

One gets $a = \sqrt[3]{\dfrac{12}{\sqrt{2}}}$ therefore $k_T = \dfrac{1}{12}\sqrt{\dfrac{2}{3}}\sqrt[3]{\dfrac{12}{\sqrt{2}}} = 0{,}1388$

Hence the tetrahedron's optimal compactness is: $\gamma_T = \dfrac{k_T}{k_{\text{Sphere}}} \approx 67{,}11\%$

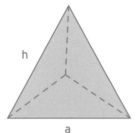

Extruded Triangle

Volume: $V = \dfrac{\sqrt{3}\, a^2\, h}{4} \Longrightarrow h = \dfrac{4\,V}{\sqrt{3}\, a^2}$ (1)

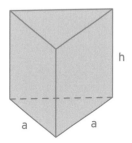

Surface area: $O = \dfrac{\sqrt{3}\, a^2}{2} + 3\,a\,h$ (2)

(1) in (2): $O\,(a) = \dfrac{\sqrt{3}\, a^2}{2} + \dfrac{12\,V}{\sqrt{3}\, a}$

(i) Determining the optimal height for a minimal surface area with a predetermined volume:

$O'_V\,(a) = \sqrt{3}\, a - \dfrac{12\,V}{\sqrt{3}\, a^2} = 0$

$\Longleftrightarrow a^3 = 4\,V$

$\quad a = \sqrt[3]{4V}$

It is obvious that the second derivation is positive.
It is therefore a minimum.

If $x = \dfrac{a}{h}$ than $h = \dfrac{a}{x} = \dfrac{4\,V}{\sqrt{3}\, a^2}$ because of (1)

$\longrightarrow x = \dfrac{\sqrt{3}\, a^3}{4\,V} = \dfrac{\sqrt{3}\, 4\,V}{4\,V} = \sqrt{3}$ after plugging in of (3)

The optimal height therefore is $h = \dfrac{a}{\sqrt{3}}$

(ii) Determination of an extruded triangle's compactness

$k_{ED} = \dfrac{V}{O} = \dfrac{\frac{1}{4}\sqrt{3}\, a^2\, h}{\dfrac{\sqrt{3}}{2}\, a^2 + 3\,a\,h}$ with $h = \dfrac{a}{\sqrt{3}}$ $\qquad k_{ED} = \dfrac{\frac{1}{4}\sqrt{3}\, a^2\, \dfrac{a}{\sqrt{3}}}{\dfrac{\sqrt{3}}{2}\, a^2 + 3\,a\, \dfrac{a}{\sqrt{3}}} = \dfrac{\frac{1}{4}\, a^3}{\dfrac{3\sqrt{3}}{2}\, a^2} = \dfrac{a}{6\sqrt{3}}$

For a certain reference volume $V = 1 = \dfrac{1}{4}\, a^3$

One gains $a = \sqrt[3]{4}$ therefore $k_{ED} = \dfrac{\sqrt[3]{4}}{6\sqrt{3}} \approx 0{,}1527$

Therefore the optimal grade of compactness for an extruded triangle is: $\gamma_{ED} = \dfrac{k_{ED}}{k_{Sphere}} \approx 73{,}9\%$

Extruded Square

Volume: $V = a^2 h \longrightarrow h = \dfrac{V}{a^2}$ (4)

Surface area: $O = 2a^2 + 4ah$ (5)

(4) in (5): $O(a) = 2a^2 + 4\dfrac{V}{a}$

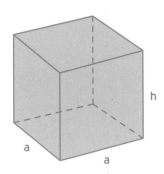

(i) Determining the optimal height for a minimal surface area with a predetermined volume:

$O'_v(a) = 4a - \dfrac{4V}{a^2} = 0$

$\Longleftrightarrow a^3 = V$

$a = \sqrt[3]{V}$

It is obvious that the second derivation is positive. It is therefore a minimum.

If now $x = \dfrac{a}{h}$ than $h = \dfrac{a}{x} = \dfrac{V}{a^2}$ because of (4)

$\longrightarrow x = \dfrac{a^3}{V} = 1$ after plugging in of (6)

The optimal height is equal to the area's side length $h = a$. The optimal square is a cube, as expected.

(ii) Determination of the cube's compactness

Volume: $V = a^3$

Surface area: $O = 6a^2$

Therefore the cube's compactness is: $k_W = \dfrac{V}{O} = \dfrac{a}{6}$

For a certain reference volume $V = 1$

One obtains $a = 1$ therefore $k_W = \dfrac{1}{6}$

Therefore the optimal grade of compactness for an extruded square is: $\gamma_W = \dfrac{k_{Cube}}{k_{Sphere}} \approx 80{,}59\%$

Extruded Pentagon

Volume: $V = \dfrac{\sqrt{25 + 10\sqrt{5}}}{4}\, a^2\, h$

$$\longrightarrow h = \dfrac{4\,V}{\sqrt{25 + 10\sqrt{5}}\; a^2} \qquad (7)$$

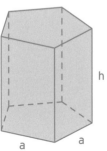

Surface area: $\quad O = \dfrac{\sqrt{25 + 10\sqrt{5}}}{2}\, a^2 + 5\,a\,h \qquad (8)$

(7) in (8): $\quad O\,(a) = \dfrac{\sqrt{25 + 10\sqrt{5}}}{2}\, a^2 + \dfrac{20\,V}{a\sqrt{25 + 10\sqrt{5}}}$

(i) Determining the optimal height for a minimal surface area with a predetermined volume:

$$O'_V\,(a) = a\sqrt{25 + 10\sqrt{5}} - \dfrac{20\,V}{a^2\sqrt{25 + 10\sqrt{5}}} = 0$$

$$\Longleftrightarrow a^3 = \dfrac{20\,V}{25 + 10\sqrt{5}} \qquad (9)$$

It is obvious that the second derivation is positive. It is therefore a minimum.

If now $\;x = \dfrac{a}{h}\;$ than $\;h = \dfrac{a}{x} = \dfrac{4\,V}{\sqrt{25 + 10\sqrt{5}}\; a^2}\;$ because of (7)

$$\longrightarrow x = \dfrac{\sqrt{25 + 10\sqrt{5}}\; a^3}{4\,V} = \dfrac{\sqrt{25 + 10\sqrt{5}}\,\dfrac{20\,V}{25 + 10\sqrt{5}}}{4\,V} = \dfrac{5}{\sqrt{25 + 10\sqrt{5}}} \qquad \text{after plugging in of (9)}$$

The optimal height therefore is $\;h = \dfrac{\sqrt{25 + 10\sqrt{5}}}{5}\, a.$

(ii) Determination of an extruded pentagon's compactness

Let $\;\alpha = \sqrt{25 + 10\sqrt{5}}$

$$k_{E\,5} = \dfrac{V}{O} = \dfrac{\dfrac{1}{20}\, a^3\, \alpha^2}{\dfrac{\alpha}{2}\, a^2 + \alpha\, a^2} \qquad \text{with} \;\; h = \dfrac{\alpha}{5}\, a$$

$$k_{E5} = \frac{\frac{1}{20} a\,\alpha}{\frac{3}{2}} = \frac{a\,\alpha}{30}$$

For a certain reference volume $V = 1 = V = \frac{1}{20} a^3 \alpha^2$

One gains $a = \sqrt[3]{\frac{20}{\alpha^2}}$ therefore $k_{E5} = \frac{\alpha^3 \sqrt{\frac{20}{\alpha^2}}}{30} = \frac{\sqrt{25+10\sqrt{5}}\;\sqrt[3]{\frac{20}{25+10\sqrt{5}}}}{30} \approx 0{,}1721$

Therefore the optimal grade of compactness for an extruded pentagram is: $\gamma_{E5} = \dfrac{k_{E5}}{k_{Sphere}} \approx 83{,}2\%$

Extruded Hexagon

Analogue to the pentagon but with a regular hexagon as the area with a base of a

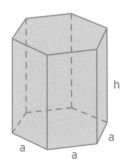

Let $\beta = \frac{3}{2}\sqrt{3}$

Volume: $V = \beta\,a^2\,h \longrightarrow h = \dfrac{V}{\beta\,a^2}$ $\qquad$ (10)

Surface area: $O = 2\,\beta\,a^2 + 6\,a\,h$ $\qquad$ (11)

(10) in (11) $\;O\,(a) = 2\,\beta\,a^2 + 6\dfrac{V}{\beta\,a}$

(i) Determining the optimal height for a minimal surface with a predetermined volume:

$$O'_v\,(a) = 4\,\beta\,a - \frac{6\,V}{\beta\,a^2} = 0$$

$$\Longleftrightarrow a^3 = \frac{6\,V}{4\,\beta^2} = \frac{2}{9}\,V \qquad (12)$$

It is obvious that the second derivation is positive. Therefore it is a minimum.

If now $x = \dfrac{a}{h}$ than $h = \dfrac{a}{x} = \dfrac{V}{\beta\,a^2}$ because of (10)

$$\longrightarrow x = \frac{\beta\,a^3}{V} = \frac{6}{4\,\beta} = \frac{1}{\sqrt{3}} \quad \text{after plugging in of (12)}$$

The optimal height therefore is $h = \sqrt{3}\,a$

(ii) Determination of an extruded hexagon's compactness

$$k_{E6} = \frac{V}{0} = \frac{\beta\, a^2\, h}{2\,\beta\, a^2 + 6\, a\, h} \quad \text{with } h = \sqrt{3}\, a$$

$$k_{E6} = \frac{\frac{3}{2}\, 3\, a^2\, a}{3\sqrt{3}\, a^2 + 6\sqrt{3}\, a^2} = \frac{a}{2\sqrt{3}}$$

For a certain reference volume $V = 1 = V = \dfrac{9}{2}\, a^3$

One gets $a = \sqrt[3]{\dfrac{2}{9}}$ therefore $k_{E6} = \dfrac{\sqrt[3]{\frac{2}{9}}}{2\sqrt{3}} \approx 0{,}1749$

Thereby the optimal grade of compactness with an extruded hexagon is: $\gamma_{E6} = \dfrac{k_{E6}}{k_{Sphere}} \approx 84{,}55\%$

Extruded Octagon

Analogue to the pentagon but with a regular octagon as the area with a base of a

if $\delta = 2(1+\sqrt{2})$

Volume: $V = \delta\, a^2\, h \longrightarrow h = \dfrac{V}{\delta\, a^2}$

Surface area: $0 = 2\,\delta\, a^2 + 8\, a\, h$

(13) in (14): $0(a) = 2\,\delta\, a^2 + 8\,\dfrac{V}{\delta\, a}$

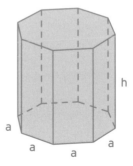

(i) Determining the optimal height for a minimal surface with a predetermined volume:

$$0'_v(a) = 4\,\delta\, a - \frac{8\,V}{\delta\, a^2} = 0$$

$$\Longleftrightarrow a^3 = \frac{2\,V}{\delta^2}$$

It is obvious that the second derivation is positive. Therefore it is a minimum.

If now $x = \dfrac{a}{h}$ than $h = \dfrac{a}{x} = \dfrac{V}{\delta\, a^2}$ because of (10)

$$\longrightarrow x = \frac{\delta\, a^3}{V} = \frac{2}{\delta} = \frac{1}{1+\sqrt{2}} \quad \text{after plugging in of (12)}$$

The optimal height therefore is $h = \dfrac{\delta}{2} a = \left(1 + \sqrt{2}\right) a.$

(ii) Determination of an extruded octagon's compactness

$$k_{E\,8} = \frac{V}{O} = \frac{\delta\, a^2\, h}{2\,\delta\, a^2 + 8\, a\, h} = \frac{\delta^2\, a^3}{4\,\delta\, a^2 + 8\, a^2\, \delta} = \frac{a\,\delta}{12} \quad \text{with (16)}$$

$$k_{E\,8} = \frac{a\left(1 + \sqrt{2}\right)}{6}$$

For a certain reference volume $V = 1 = \dfrac{1}{2}\,\delta^2\, a^3$

one gains $a = \sqrt[3]{\dfrac{2}{\delta^2}} = \sqrt[3]{\dfrac{1}{2\left(1+\sqrt{2}\right)^2}}$ therefore $k_{E\,6} = \left(1 + \sqrt{2}\right)\dfrac{\sqrt[3]{\dfrac{1}{2\left(1+\sqrt{2}\right)^2}}}{6} \approx 0{,}1775$

Thereby the optimal grade of compactness with an extruded octagon is: $\gamma_{E\,8} = \dfrac{k_{E\,8}}{k_{Sphere}} \approx 85{,}8\%$

Cylinder

Volume: $V = \pi\, r^2\, h \longrightarrow h = \dfrac{V}{\pi\, r^2}$ $\qquad\qquad$ (17)

Surface Area $O = 2\,\pi\, r^2 + 2\,\pi\, r\, h$ $\qquad\qquad$ (18)

(17) in (18): $O\left(r\right) = 2\,\pi\, r^2 + 2\,\dfrac{V}{r}$

(i) Determining the optimal height for a minimal surface with a predetermined volume:

$$O'_v\left(r\right) = 4\,\pi\, r - \frac{2\,V}{r^2} = 0$$

$$2\,\pi\, r = \frac{V}{r^2} \qquad\qquad (12)$$

$$r^3 = \frac{V}{2\,\pi}$$

It is obvious that the second derivation is positive. Therefore it is a minimum.

If now $x = \dfrac{r}{h}$ than $h = \dfrac{r}{x} = \dfrac{V}{\pi\, r^2}$ because of (17)

$$\longrightarrow x = \frac{r^3\,\pi}{V} = \frac{1}{2} \quad \text{after plugging in (19)}$$

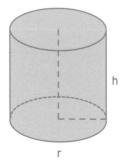

The optimal height therefore is twice as big as the radius.

(ii) Determination of a cylinder's compactness

$$k_Z = \frac{V}{0} = \frac{\pi\, r^2\, h}{2\,\pi\,(r^2 + r\,h)} \quad \text{with } h = 2\,r$$

$$k_Z = \frac{2\,\pi\, r^3}{6\,\pi\, r^2} = \frac{r}{3}$$

For a certain reference volume $\quad V = 1 = 2\,\pi\, r^3$

one gains $\quad r^3 = \dfrac{1}{2\,\pi} \quad$ therefore $\quad k_Z = \dfrac{1}{3}\sqrt[3]{\dfrac{1}{2\,\pi}}$

Thereby the compactness of a cylinder is: $\quad \gamma_Z = \dfrac{k_{Cylinder}}{k_{Sphere}} = \sqrt[3]{\dfrac{2}{3}} \approx 87{,}36\%$

The principle of a tumbler

A tumbler regularly has a rounded bottom, the centre of gravity lies very far in the lower part. Every change in position raises the centre of gravity and makes the tumbler get upright its own due to gravity. If the tumbler has a hemispherical bottom the centre of gravity has to lie below the sphere's centre.

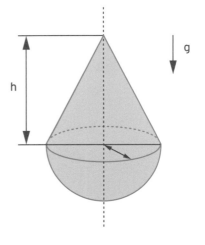

GLOSSARY

ABS

ABS means acrylonitrile butadiene styrene and is a synthetic terpolymer. The synthetic material is made from three different monomers and belongs to the amorphous thermoplastics. ABS synthetic materials are fabricates by graft polymerization in commercial proceedings or through blending the finished polymers. ABS's characteristics are a strong surface hardness and impact resistance and that it can easily be coated with metals or polymers.

Anglepoise

The "Anglepoise task light 1933/34" is a task light designed around the year 1930 by the English automotive engineer George Carwadine (1887 – 1948). With this model the industrial designer made spring loaded lamps popular that could be moved in every direction. To design the light made for workspaces he developed a new way of construction inspired by the human arm: He fixed the lampshade on a flexible long arm. Springs at the joints balance the lamp by using the interaction between traction and counteraction. The Anglepoise (originating from the two words angle and poise) today is the most copied task light and is a classic in industrial design.

Art Deco

Art Deco (originating from the French l'art écoratif = decorative art) is a collective term for a style of the 1920s to 1940s summarizing architecture, poster art, photography, and overall the industrial design of everyday objects. Art Deco succeeded Art Nouveau, seized its conscious-ness for forms but at the same time presented a new industrial design oriented around the new era of machines. Abstract and elegant forms, a very ornamental style, symmetries and the use of expensive materials like noble woods, ivory, chrome and crystal played an exceeding role for the Art Deco repertoire of forms. Especially in jewelry and furniture design it was marked in the production of only very small quantities. The style's simplicity also shaped the industrial design and the fabrication of lower quality mass products like home appliances and fashion accessories. The name Art Deco has been used since the 1960s in relation to the Parisian arts and crafts fair under the same name in the year 1925.

Art Nouveau
Art Nouveau is an art style of the turn-of-the-century between the 19th and 20th century. Other names for this special style are Modern Style, Modernisme, Stile Liberty, Reformstil or Wiener Secession, in Russia it is called Stil Modern and the French also used the term Fin de siècle. In German speaking countries, the Netherlands and Nordic countries often enough the term Jugendstil is used, named after the Munich illustrated cultural journal "Jugend" – a term relatively unbiased shaped through modern art history. When first mentioned in 1901 the Jugend- or Secessions Style was used by some German magazines (like "Decorative Kunst" where Hermann Muthesius and Julius Meier-Graefe authored articles) as a critical label to describe a modern popularization. The authors thought it to be a caricature of new forms made famous by artists like Henry van de Velde, a caricature imitating these artists' work in a cheap arts-and-crafts mass production. Decorative, curved lines, floral ornaments and an abandonment of symmetry were the main features of Art Nouveau. But even with that classification one should not forget that Art Noveau was no unified movement, as the term today might imply. It is a conglomerate of very different tendencies all over Europe, that were at least united in the rejection of Historicism, the up to this point then well-established method of copying historically passed on patterns of form and design.

Many artistic programs and manifestos refer to Art Nouveau. Today it also means overall artistic concepts like the Palais Stoclet in Brussels that unites exterior and interior design to an entity. Art Nouveau is the long sought after mergence of art and life, the reintegration of art into every-day-life in the sense of an artistic re-design of every-day items giving the decorative art a bigger importance. At this point Art Nouveau follows a concept Historicism had already pledged alliance to in making the term Gesamtkunstwerk (synthesis of the arts) a main programme. It was a programmatic counter project to the aloofness and isolation of auratic artwork in the spheres of fine arts. But functionality and the expression of function was also part of the programme, the function of a building for example should already be acknowledged in its outer design. Symmetrical and axial allocations were no longer a must be, facades should far more follow the conception of space as presented in the layout. For many artists of the Art Nouveau movement it was essential to renounce from historical construction forms and search for new ways in design, architecture, arts and crafts. They furthermore continued the essential debate of the 19th century, the question of "what is a modern style? What is the style of our times?".

Arts and Crafts Movement
Arts and Crafts was a reform movement originating in England. It was an answer to the industrialization and the mechanical and soulless production. The movement promoted modest and convenient forms in industrial design but also asked for a return to traditional virtues, the beauty of handcrafted quality. The Arts and Crafts movement emerged in the middle of the 19th century and was essentially shaped by William Morris and John Ruskin. They wanted to unite arts and crafts according to the model of the Middle Age guilds, they criticized the loss of individuality and knowledge concerning traditional techniques as well as the enslavement of workers in factories. The socially motivated movement organized spectacular exhibitions and had its golden age between 1870 and 1920. The aesthetic and social perception of the Arts and Crafts movement was the base for a modern industrial design. It gave impulse to other artists movements like the Art Nouveau or Bauhaus.

Banal Design
A term to criticise an overdone design, industrial designer and architect Alessandro Mendini used it to put the industrial design of ordinary items into focus and stylise trivialities as high culture. Things for every day use like clothes pegs, flatirons and carpet sweepers are accentuated with decorative elements, alienated or put together in new ways. In 1980 Mendini organized an exhibition for the Venice Biennale together with Paolo Navone, Franco Raggi and Daniela Puppa. Its title: "L'Ogetto Banale". Beyond that banal design is also used for the industrial design of mass consumer goods, that cannot please consumer's needs accordingly.

Bauhaus
Walter Gropius founded Bauhaus as a new form of art school in Weimar in 1919. The school moved to Dessau in 1925 and to Berlin in 1932 where it was closed down under the Nazi regime in 1933. The idea was to combine art and handcraft in education, to bring together liberal and applied arts. Teachers at the academy were among the most prominent artists of their time. They developed the base for architectural science, new pedagogic concepts and aesthetic norms for industrial design. After the school was closed down many artists emigrated to the U.S., Great Britain, France and Russia. The cultural heritage of Bauhaus influenced art, architecture and design for years to come. The reception of the Bauhaus modernity continues into the present age and in industrial design it is still a synonym for factual, intelligent design.

Bionics

Bionics is a science researching nature and the principles and methods it is based on to convey them to technology and transfer them into a concrete use. It is an interdisciplinary method uniting natural science and engineering as well as architecture, philosophy and industrial design. The term bionics was coined in 1960 by the American Air Force major, Jack E. Steele during a conference in Dayton, Ohio. Bionics is a word that emerged from the front and back syllables of the two words biology and technics. Bionics is more than just copying nature: Bionics is inspired by constructions, proceedings and development principles of biological systems but changes these insights for a technical use. Industrial designers therefore can for example develop intelligent products, with reduced material and energy consumption.

CAD

Computer Aided Design (short CAD) was at first only used as a term for computer work in technical drawing. Instead of working on a drawing board, construction plans were made as a two-dimensional flat drawing that could be viewed on a monitor or printed on paper sheets. In product design CAD can today be used to create three-dimensional volume models, that can be virtually moved and from which two-dimensional drawings could be extrapolated and created. CAD-programmes allow controlling production machines for technical objects directly with a computer.

Corporate Identity

Corporate Identity (in short: CI) is an important term in marketing: How would a company like to present itself and be perceived by customers? CI is the organized interaction of appearance, communication and behavior. The concept presumes that companies like people have a personality and identity. The company's personality develops if the visual appearance and the way of acting become an integral whole. Parts of the corporate identity are the visual identity (Corporate Design), the behavior toward the public, consumers, suppliers and staff (Corporate Behavior), the inner and outer communication (Corporate Communication), the company's philosophy and culture (Corporate Philosophy, Corporate Culture) and a company specific language (Corporate Language). Industrial design can support the corporate identity, for example when it is used to represent a company's guiding principles.

Design

In the beginning design meant a drawn – designed – or plastic draft (sketch, model). Designing is a process where humans acquire an object through a deed, make it useful and change it. The designer influences the environment willingly, to change it in a certain way. Today the collective term design stands for the complete origination process of industrially manufactured serial products from the planning stage to the actual design. The better term therefore is product design or industrial design. In industrial design the term means a creative process in which a product gains its visible form, its appearance. An industrial designer has to mediate between his client's wishes and needs and those of the later users. A designer takes practical and aesthetic aspects into account as well as production methods and economic aspects. As much as the process the object itself can be called a design. The term design originates from the Latin word "designare" which means to designate or to depict the outline or shape.

Draft

A draft is an analytic and creative achievement and the result of solving a problem. It is a strategy of thinking to overcome complicated and vast situations. In art and industrial design drafting is a key activity and a preparation for the elaboration of the later developed object. In industrial design the draft is the base for the realization of a product. It starts with a preliminary idea. The ides will become more concrete when sketched on paper, exemplified as a model, processed and in the end realized or discarded. A draft is the description of a purpose in words and pictures. The word to draft has its origin in figurative language and means nothing else but to sketch or to draw a picture.

Ergonomics

Ergonomics (legitimacy of work) is the science of the working human being and the adjustment of working conditions to human needs. One task is the humane design of workspaces (office, factory, household), a second the development of easy and comfortable to handle products wherever humans work with machines and tools (automotive, computer, telephone, etc.). Ergonomic product design creates products that can be used intuitively and without any danger. It creates conditions to guarantee an efficient and accurate workmanship for ensuring a worker's working capacity and health as well as promoting quality of living.

Form

The form describes the outer, vivid shape. It is the bearer of an object's visual, aesthetic and symbolic aspects. Its counterparts are the practical functions like ergonomic requirements, handling and safety. Industrial design always moves between both poles – form and function – forming an inseparable entity. According to content-related tasks, zeitgeist and the motives and methods of a designer the functionality (Bauhaus, Hochschule für Gestaltung, Ulm) or the form (for example Memphis) outweigh the other. The design principle "form follows function" was an hard and fast rule for many years but strictness declined since the 1970s when the principle was changed in sentences like "form follows fun", "form follow emotion" or "form follows fiction".

Functionalism

When speaking of functionalism one means that a design orientates itself on a building or object's practical and useful aspects, therefore forcing aesthetic aspects to retreat behind purpose and practicality. The term refers to modern architecture and industrial design of the early 20th century. Louis Henry Sullivan's "form follows function" became a professed programme at that time. The idea behind this was that the beauty in architecture and design reveals itself in the current functionality. From this a counter movement to historicism began to develop that preferred a rational style, emphasized purpose and construction as well as geometrical forms and square angles. In Germany this principle reached its peak after the Second World War and was universal for industrial design until the 1980s. The creations at the Hochschule für Gestaltung, Ulm or the designs of Braun chief designer Dieter Rahms display a functional and factual industrial design.

Haptics

Haptics is the science of the tactile sense and plays an important role in industrial design next to handling and ergonomics. To achieve an enjoyable and secure grip the Braun company for example developed a special synthetic material for their razors. The sense of touch is as important as visual, acoustic or olfactory senses, to grasp an object's features and judge a product design: Smooth surfaces seem to be cold and repellent, rough materials seem sharp and brittle.

Health Rate

In quality checks the health rate describes the ratio between the count of flawless products to those with a deficiency. The quotient shows how many mistakes are made during the production. If for example one finds a fault in only one of ten products the health rate is 90 %.

Industrial Design, Product Design

Industrial Design or Product Design is a collective name for the origination of planning and designing industrially fabricated serial products. An industrial designer does not create individual and unique items but products that can be fabricated in mass production. Most times he works on behalf of a client and looks at the possibility of fabricating the product mechanically. The customer's expectations play an important role as well. Industrial design works in the field between art, engineering science, ergonomics and marketing.

Interface Design

Interface Design is a discipline, that engages in the communication processes between humans and computers and in the visual conceptualization of interfaces. Interface design researches the conditions, aims and obstacles of interactions between man and machine and optimizes operator interfaces. The human user should be enabled to work optimally and profitably with digital devices and services with appropriate action steps. The work of interface designers in parts overlaps with those of interaction design, which researches an artifact's utilization scenarios. Interface designers work in the fields of internet communication, software, web and product design.

Interior Design

Interior Design is a branch of architecture and engages in shaping, furnishing and decorating living and work spaces. Quality in atmosphere and psychological well-being are as important as technical and functional aspects. In comparison with industrial design that always has to consider the ability to produce something in a series, an interior designer mostly designs prototypes and conceptualizes individual solutions.

Low Volume Production

Products of the same kind fabricated in small quantities are parts of a low volume production or small scale series. The number of copies varies between three and a hundred. In comparison with industrial mass production the products are fabricated for a very small market and in small quantities. The production is far more cost-intensive. Low volume productions can be found in industrial design as well as in crafts. Even a "limited edition" has far bigger quantities than a small-scale series.

Microarchitecture

Microarchitecture describes small objects in tabletop design that were developed out of an architectural form language. Those items fabricated for tables play with the scales and dimensions of buildings and with architectural details like pillars and gables. Alberto Alessi initiated the mutual fertilization of architecture and product design when he developed the project "Tea and Coffee Piazza" in 1979: He asked eleven architects to design tea and coffee sets that could be arranged like an architectonic ensemble on a tray – the piazza.

Minimal Art, Minimalism

Minimal art had its origin in the U.S. of the 1960s as a tendency towards abstraction in modern art. The artists intended to reduce the form to its primary structure. The word minimalism relates to plastics in the first place. Clear geometrical forms, often in serial repetition, the use of industrial finished products (tiles, neon tubes, steel framings) and a tendency towards depersonalization and objectivity were the characteristics of minimal art. The artists refrained from decorating accessories and reduced their form language to a base structure. Their objects have a distinct order that alerts the viewer to room functional aspects. In industrial design and architecture minimalism gained accepted in the 1980s with the principle "less is more". Buildings and objects were reduced to their essentials, to simple, clear and often geometrical structures.

Modelmaking

In modelmaking a real or planned example is recreated as a three-dimensional, physical object. The model is lifelike and rescaled in a smaller size, simplified or is used as a model to create a negative mould. To create and test functional parts, tools or display models there are different production methods like stereolithography, multi-jet modelling and selective laser treatment.

Multi-Jet Modelling

Multi-jet modelling (MJM) is a manufacturing process in the field of rapid prototyping. The existing CAD data is implemented directly into work pieces without manual interference. The chemical process resembles stereolithography: materials are UV-sensitive photopolymers. The model is built up through a push button and nozzles, similarly to the principle of an inkjet printer.

No-Design

The term "No-design" was used for the first time by industrial designer Jasper Morrison in the 1980s. No-design products are the result of a sophisticated design process but do not point out their value obviously. Instead they take practical and modest items as an example, things that seem familiar and indispensible but are normally not recognized very much when used. Minimalistic design like Jasper Morrison's "Chair" and objects made by Mondo are good examples for No-design. Sometimes daily used items of banal design are also named No-design.

OEM

is an original equipment manufacturer, (the original manufacturer of products or components for a product, which may be resold by another company.) The manufacturer produces products or components by itself, but doesn't distribute and market them under its own label. Products or components may be marketed and distributed on behalf of the customer's label.

Organic Design

Organic Design is an industrial design style that makes organic and flowing forms borrowed from nature the base of design. Curved lines, dynamic rounding and powerful curvatures form a contrast to a geometrical and factual style represented in Functionalism. Attempts to find more organic and natural forms have always played a part in industrial design: in 1946 with the Vespa scooter Piaggio built a streamlined vehicle body. And in 1950 Charles Eames designed the fiberglass armchair "Dax" with an organically formed seat shell. The golden era for organic forms were the 1970s and their synthetic plastic furniture. Since 2000 automotive design has a tendency to flowing forms – for example the newly designed Mini Cooper. Design drafts of industrial designers like Ron Arad, Luigi Colani, Massimo Iosa Ghini, Ross Lovegrove and Philippe Starck are obviously influenced by organic forms and design.

Pop Art

Pop Art or Popular Art has its origin in the 1950s in England and the U.S. and became the internationally leading form of art in the 1960s. Pop Art artists turned towards banal items of every day life and consumption products (advertisements, comics, trivial magazines) marking our mass society. They ironically pointed out modern human's purpose in life. They took up Dadaistic techniques and intentions and demanded that art had to fit into the sociological context of its time. Roy Lichtenstein, Andy Warhol or Tom Wesselmann radicalized these tendencies by using the techniques and effects of advertising graphics and in raising mass media images to iconic status presented through a variety of series. Pop Art also inspired industrial design. Pop Art motives and its playful attitude can for example be found in the works of De Pas/D'Urbino/Lomazzi, Elio Fiorucci or Peter Murdoch.

Postmodernism

The term Postmodernism is an overall term for a pluralistic style and way of thinking that distances itself from the dogmatic conceived modernity and its aesthetic proceedings. Postmodernism allows different forms and possibilities to coexist equally. In architecture Postmodernism first made an impact in the 1960s as a style that gave new life to old forms (pillars, gables) in a playful way and combined them with new shapes. In the 1980s the new extroverted industrial design benefited in form and content from postmodernist architecture. Architects like Hans Hollein, Michael Graves and Robert Venturi experimented with this style in their furniture designs, many impulses came from Italy. Architects and designers came together in new studios like "Alchimia" (1976 -81) and "Memphis" (1981 – 88) to declare their new programme. In their work they borrowed styles from various historico-cultural epochs, used colors and decors and an anti-functional shaping.

Postprocessing

This term describes after-treatment of individual manufacturing steps like casting, forging, welding etc. by using chemical or physical processes like sand blasting, acid etching or anodizing to optimize and complete the result.

Prototype

The prototype (from Greece prototypos = archetype) in engineering and industrial design denotes the test model of a new development. It is a functional or simplified true to size exemplar of a component or product that in look and function matches the end product. A prototype is the most essential step in industrial design because it can be used to test practical features and characteristics. When a prototype is made directly before the start of a serial production often enough a null series follows as a last practicality test.

PU, PUR

Polyurethane (in short PU or PUR) combines a group of synthetic materials that according to their starting compound have different properties. They all have in common a reaction of two chemical elements – a superior alcohol (polyalcohol) and an isocyanate. They were discovered in 1937 through polyaddition of a polyol (polyalcohol) with a polyisocyanate. PU synthetic materials are often used for plastic foams, for example sponges, mattresses or expanding foams for isolations as well as in lacquer and glue. Because of their various features they are an ideal material for industrial design.

PVC

Polyvinylchloride (short: PVC) is a synthetic material with a varying elasticity according to additional substances and can therefore be adjusted to very different fields of application. Next to tenacity and elasticity additives can improve the resistance to light, temperature and weather as well as changing the glance. In brittle and hard consistency the material is for example used for pipes, gutters or hard protective cases, in soft consistency as garden hose or flooring. The synthetic material is also used as PVC paste for coating textiles (rain coat) or foam material (upholstered furniture).

Redesign

Redesign means the creative revision of an existing product to gradually improve its practical value for users. The design group "Alchimia" used redesign in the 1980s to criticise the design philosophy of Functionalism. Next to everyday items (Banal Design) Italian designers like Alessandro Mendini also used well-known works to parody them. Mendini for example played with icons of modern industrial design like the Thonet chair or Marcel Breuer's "Wassily Chair" and adorned them with patterns and objects.

Re-edition

The term re-edition especially in furniture and textile design means the reinvestment of older industrial design products according to original plans. It attempts to get as close as possible to the original. In the 1960s a couple of firms bought the right to re-edit furniture classics while the originals were mostly displayed in museums or in private collections. In 1962 the Thonet firm re-edited Marcel Breuer furniture. Other manufacturers like Cassina, Knoll and Zanote made re-editions of Le Corbusier, Charles Rennie Mackintosh, Ludwig Mies van der Rohe or Guiseppe Terragni.

Selective-Laser-Sintering

Selective-laser-sintering procedures (SLS) are used in prototype building to fabricate models and exemplary components, whose structures are created layer after layer. Base materials are granules made of synthetics, sand, metal or ceramic. The object emerges when the layers are molten or sintered into the powder bed with a laser. The laser follows the exact contours beforehand constructed in a CAD dataset.

Stereolithography

Stereolithography (STL or STA) is another computer-based process in the field of rapid proto-typing (or rapid manufacturing). It can be used for producing prototypes, moulding templates or industrial models. In stereolitography a light-curing resin (photopolymer) is brought to poly-merisation with a laser and therefore conveyed from a liquid to a solid state. Out of the data of a CAD model the object emerges layer by layer.

Streamline

The term streamline emerged in the 1920s in the environment of aerodynamics and the inves-tigation of air resistance in trains, automobiles and aeroplanes. With developing streamlined vehicle bodies engineers tried to optimize them aerodynamically. In architecture and industrial design streamline is used since the 1930s especially in the US and became a part of Art Deco. Streamline design was a synonym for speed and orientation towards the future. It emphasises curved, dynamic forms and a long, horizontal linehaul. After the Second World War streamline design was used for the scooter Vespa. In the late 1980s it became a famous stylistic device for example in the designs of Massimo Iosa Ghini or Marc Newson.

Tabletop Design

Tabletop design is an overall term for table accessories of all kinds. Next to cutlery, dishes, mills and ménages it includes decorations like vases, table lamps or candlesticks. Manufacturers like the Swedish company Kosta Boda, the Italian firm Alessi as well as Germany's WMF specialize in tabletop design.

Unicum

An unicum is an item planned as a single copy. In contrast to a prototype that precedes an industrial serial production, there is no duplication or copy of an unicum. Unique copies are typical for handicraft. They are normally handmade originals, designed especially for one person and according to this person's wishes. Compared to industrial design production costs and technical conditions mostly play no role at all for a unique copy.

Target Group

Target group names an interest group, a group of like-minded people a vendor sees as potential customers (persons, firms etc.) for the product or service. Every advertising effort is directed towards them. There are many different concepts of how to recognise and form this group that are discussed in literature under the topic of target group analysis.

A survey of important foundations

Idea	Innovation Novelty Necessity Producibility Commercial potential
Functionality	Effectivity Efficiency Practicability Interoperability with surrounding products Physical ergonomics Mental ergonomics
Aesthetics	Consistency Proportions Design grid Symmetry Clarity Regularity Color combination Material combination Product graphic and typography Surface character and haptics Authenticity Production quality
Economy and Ecology	Choice of materials in regard to resources Choice of materials in regard to energy consumption Choice of materials in regard to stress and function Choice of materials in regard to environmental friendliness Choice of materials in regard to geometry Material efficiency in regard to statics Production costs with regard to from and material Production costs in regard to assembly Health rate Sustainability and obsolescence
Marketing	Equivalence and consistency Independence Product character in harmony with the brand Product character in harmony with function Product character in harmony with the target group Emotionalism

16x

red dot design award | Design Zentrum Nordrhein-Westfalen
2014 supraGuide ECO | 2014 supraGuide MULTI | 2013 File/it | 2013 Milli | 2013 Locko
2012 IVDR Verbatim | 2012 USB Kingston | 2012 Square HDD | 2012 Mobile SQ | 2012 Digipipe
2012 Handycan | 2012 Loopo | 2012 Art Detector | 2010 Neolog OS | 2009 Steward
2006 Neolog A24 II

3x

red dot design award - best of the best | Design Zentrum Nordrhein-Westfalen
2013 Zipper | 2010 USB-Clip | 2009 USB-Clip

6x

iF design award | International Design Forum
2014 supraGuide MULTI | 2013 Data Traveler | 2012 Hard SQ | 2011 Neolog OS
2011 Neolog OS Packaging | 2009 Neolog Europe Internetpräsenz

2x

iF design award gold | International Design Forum
2012 Mobile SQ | 2012 Hard SQ

2x

GOOD Design Award Japan | G-Mark JIDPO
2010 USB-Clip | 2006 Neolog A24 II

10x

GOOD Design Award USA | Chicago Athenaeum Museum of Architecture and Design
2012 Zipper | 2012 Locko | 2012 Freecom SQ Mobile Drive | 2011 Milli Motal and Pestle
2011 Loopo USB Flash | 2011 Timeout Glove | 2010 Neolog OS | 2010 USB-Clip
2009 NO K.O. | 2006 Cha Cha

3x

German Design Award | Rat für Formgebung German Design Council
2014 Zipper | 2014 supraGuide ECO | 2013 USB-Clip

11x

Designpreis Deutschland – Nominierung | Rat für Formgebung German Design Council
2014 supraGuide MULTI | 2013 Loopo | 2013 Timeout Glove | 2013 Sq hard drive
2012 USB-Clip | 2011 NO K.O. | 2011 USB-Clip | 2011 Neolog Europe Internetpräsenz
2010 Neolog OS | 2009 Cha Cha | 2007 Neolog A-24 II

2x

Focus Open | Internationaler Designpreis Baden-Württemberg
2011 Neolog OS | 2011 USB-Clip

Arman Emami founded Emamidesign in 2005, and currently directs the company from its office in Berlin-Mitte. Since its establishment, Emamidesign has developed over 41 products, patented 23 of them and won 54 international awards. Emamidesign is at the top of the international red dot rankings for the best design concepts.

www.emamidesign.de